INFANTRY ACES OF THE REICH

GORDON WILLIAMSON

ARMS AND
ARMOUR

This book is dedicated to Hans Sturm,
a gallant soldier and true friend.

Arms and Armour Press
A Cassell Imprint
Villiers House, 41–47 Strand, London WC2N 5JE.

Distributed in the USA by Sterling Publishing Co. Inc.,
387 Park Avenue South, New York, NY 10016-8810.

Distributed in Australia by Capricorn Link (Australia) Pty.
Ltd, P.O. Box 665, Lane Cove, New South Wales 2066.

British Library Cataloguing in Publication Data
Williamson, Gordon
Infantry aces of the Reich
1. Army operations. History
I. Title
940.5413530922
ISBN 1-85409-065-8

Jacket illustration courtesy of Brian L. Davis.

Designed and edited by DAG Publications Ltd. Designed by
David Gibbons; edited by Michael Boxall; typeset by Ronset
Typesetters, Darwen, Lancashire; camerawork by M&E
Reproductions, North Fambridge, Essex; printed and
bound in Great Britain by Mackays of Chatham, Kent.

Contents

Introduction	**11**
Acknowledgements	**13**
Badges and Awards of the Combat Soldier	**15**
The Men	**27**
1939–40	29
1941	47
1942	55
1943	71
1944	93
1945	121
Appendixes	**141**
Appendix 1. Comparative Ranks	143
Appendix 2. Unit Structure	145
Glossary	**147**
Bibliography	**149**
Index	**151**

Introduction

I n the fifty years which have elapsed since the outbreak of the Second World War, countless books have been written about the daring deeds of the war heroes of all the participating nations. Those written during the war were, understandably, heavily biased to boost the morale of personnel on the home front; books written in more recent times have been more objective. As old hatreds have faded, virulent anti-German propaganda has all but disappeared and, while the excesses committed by some are still abhorred, the magnificent fighting qualities of the German soldier during the war are now more widely acknowledged. On the German side, reluctance to discuss wartime experiences has faded, and as many former German soldiers become willing to open up and discuss their military careers, much important new photographic and documentary material has emerged.

Understandably, perhaps, the vast bulk of the biographical material which has appeared in the past has related to the famous General, the accomplished Sea Captain or the successful Fighter Ace. The image of the handsome, dashing young fighter pilot in his smart uniform implies a degree of glamour which most soldiers who fought on the ground would find totally alien. Certainly the mud-caked infantryman slogging his way through the mire of the Russian Front would hardly have seen military life as glamorous, and, without in any way belittling the achievements of the fighter pilot, there are few examples of personal heroism which could match those performed by the members of that major contributor to the success of any army – the infantry, known to the Germans as *Der Königin der Waffe* (Queen of Arms), to the British the 'P.B.I.' (Poor Bloody Infantry), the often scorned infantryman – in almost every Army the infantryman is known by an uncomplimentary if affectionate title, stubble-hoppers, grunts, cannon-fodder – is the soldier who is most likely to come into direct physical contact with the enemy. Not for him the impersonal target such as the tank or the enemy aircraft. His target was the flesh and blood enemy soldier and in terrifying hand-to-hand combat the infantry of the Wehrmacht was to prove itself second to none. Many acts of supreme heroism were performed by these 'common soldiers' yet few of these men have become household names even in their own land, indeed few people will have ever heard of most of them.

Through my contacts among surviving Knight's Cross winners, I have assembled a selection of cases where the award of the Knight's Cross of the Iron Cross was made, not for leadership, or for success in destroying a particular number of enemy tanks or ships, or aircraft, but for acts of great personal gallantry. The cases presented here are those which, had they been performed by an Allied soldier, might well have attracted the award of the Victoria Cross for a British serviceman, or the Medal of Honor for an American. The fact that these German soldiers fought for a regime which is now held in abhorrence is irrelevant. Heroism must be considered objectively. A brave man is a brave man whatever cause he fights for. These are soldiers who, when the chips were down, put their lives on the line and in total contempt of personal danger, continued to fight when any lesser man would have considered the situation lost.

No famous generals or field marshals will be found here. These are ordinary soldiers from the infantry and its support arms, the majority of whom were other ranks, NCOs or at most junior officers at the time of their award winning exploits. In most cases the soldiers included in this book are still alive at the time of writing, and have personally contributed photographs and details of their military exploits.

NOTE. Although the term infantry has been used, this book includes paratroopers, pioneers, grenadiers, etc. In effect, these are men who fought on the ground and were, when in combat, basically foot soldiers.

Edinburgh
Autumn 1990

Acknowledgements

In the production of any work of this type it is inevitable that the assistance of others with an interest in the subject will be sought. This work is no exception. A number of surviving Knight's Cross winners have graciously given information and photographs from their personal albums. The majority of these are previously unpublished. I am also grateful to the surviving next of kin of some of the soldiers included, who also kindly donated photographs and information. The names of these contributors are listed here, and to them I extend my grateful thanks.

I must make special mention, however, of my good friend Hans Sturm, whose own military exploits are covered in the pages of this work. As soon as he was informed about the preparation of this book he expressed his eager willingness to assist. Many Knight's Cross winners have been pestered dreadfully over the years by a number of inquirers ranging from genuine students of military history to muckraking journalists and so called collectors trying to buy their coveted decorations. It is understandable therefore that many Knight's Cross winners are suspicious of any approaches for information, and many such requests simply go unanswered. The benefit of having Hans approach these people on my behalf has been inestimable. An approach from a fellow Knight's Cross winner will almost always bring a polite and helpful reply. Having devoted much time and effort to assisting with this work, his contribution has been of great help and is gratefully acknowledged.

If the average former German soldier is often wary of any sort of media reportage, the former soldiers of the Waffen-SS are even more reluctant, having seen so many of their comrades badly treated by the lurid stories of the gutter press over the past 45 years. I consider myself, therefore, most fortunate that my good friend Hein Springer (who himself won the Knight's Cross for an heroic action in capturing the bridge over the River Don at Rostov in 1941), a former SS-Sturmbann-führer in the élite Leibstandarte, has willingly assisted me in this and previous works.

The true reward in producing a book such as this is not in any financial gain that may result, but in the genuine and lasting friendships made with many of these gallant soldiers during the course of my research: Wolfgang von Bostell, Rudolf Donth, Willi Fey, Ferdinand Foltin, Eduard Hug, Hans Hauser, Hans Hinrich Karck, Heinrich Keese, Michael Pössinger, Gustav-Peter Reber, Bruno Sassen, Hans Sturm, Remi Schrynen, Alfred Schneidereit, Karl Ullrich, Wilhelm Wegener, Franz Weber, Martin Steglich.

Badges and Awards of the Combat Soldier

The following small selection of badges are brought to the reader's attention because they are the combat awards most commonly worn by the German infantryman and are to be seen in many of the photographs within this book. These are badges awarded only for combat actions and, unlike some other decorations such as campaign awards, could not be acquired merely by 'being there'. Even such common awards as the Infantry Assault Badge, the award which usually followed soon after the soldiers' 'baptism of fire' were worn with great pride.

In addition, the soldiers covered in this book will all be seen to wear the coveted Knight's Cross of the Iron Cross as well as the Iron Crosses First and Second Class. These are covered in depth in the author's previous works *The Iron Cross, an Illustrated History* and *Knights of the Iron Cross*, both published by Blandford Press, and so will only receive brief coverage here in order to identify their purposes for any reader unfamiliar with German military decorations.

As will be noted from the photographic content of this book, the German soldier, unlike his Allied counterpart, wore virtually all his military decorations at all times, even in the thick of combat. A vast industry existed in wartime Germany to produce the wide range of awards and insignia required by the Third Reich's military and para-military organizations. Generally speaking, when the award of a badge was made, the piece was pinned to the recipient's tunic by one of his superior officers, he was handed the award certificate, and the protective wrapper for the badge was simply thrown away. However, the recipient could, if desired, purchase as many extra examples of the badge as he liked. By producing his award certificate at any retail outlet controlled by the *Leistungsgemeinschaft deutscher Ordenshersteller* (Association of German Order manufacturers), he could purchase a wide range of examples of his award, in materials ranging from zinc to hallmarked silver depending on how much he wished to spend, contained in anything from a cellophane bag to a luxury velvet-lined case. A considerable number of firms produced these awards and many marked their produce with either the name of the firm, a firm's logo, or a code number allocated to the firm. These marks, found on the reverse of the badge or on the pin fitting, are of no great significance as almost every known maker's mark has been copied by forgers. The quality of current forgeries of German military awards is so high, complete with all relevant maker's hallmarks, presentation cases and even award certificates on aged paper, that many collectors of long standing have given up interest in the subject. Indeed the purchase of any type of Second World War German militaria is an extremely risky business.

The Infantry Assault Badge (*Infanterie Sturmabzeichen*)

The single most important and widely distributed combat infantry award was the Infantry Assault Badge. Instituted on 20 December 1939 by Generaloberst von Brauchitsch, Commander-in-Chief of the Army, the badge consists of a vertical oval wreath of oakleaves topped by a stylized Wehrmacht eagle with folded wings, clutching a swastika in its talons. In the centre of the badge, lying diagonally from right to left, is an accurate representation of a Mauser Mar98k carbine, the standard weapon of the German infantryman, with fixed bayonet. The badge measures 63mm × 49mm. The first awards were made in April 1940.

The badge was produced in two forms, with silvered finish for infantry proper, and a bronze version introduced in June 1940 for motorized infantry. The award was designed and first produced by the Berlin firm of C. E. Juncker, one of the foremost manufacturers of military awards during the Third Reich. The Infantry Assault Badge was manufactured in a variety of metals ranging from finely silver-plated bronze in early awards, to zinc or pot-metal later in the war. Badges could be solid cast or stamped, or semi-hollow die struck. Generally featuring a vertical hinged pin on the reverse, occasional examples are encountered with screwback fittings. The badge was worn on the left breast pocket.

In order to qualify for the badge, the prospective recipient had to have taken part in a minimum of three individual infantry assault actions on three separate occasions. Usually authorized by the soldier's regimental commander, the badge was accompanied by a certificate of entitlement. These existed in a wide variety of forms and sizes, often locally produced. Some were simple typewritten sheets of paper; others were elaborately illuminated. Normally actually pinned to the recipient's tunic during the award ceremony, the badge came from the manufacturer in a paper or cellophane envelope with the title of the award, *Infanterie Sturmabzeichen*, normally printed in black gothic characters thereon. These packets were usually thrown away, and although not particularly valuable, are now becoming rather scarce.

The Infantry Assault Badge can be clearly seen in the photograph of Gustav-Peter Reber and Remi Schrynen.

The General Assault Badge
(*Allgemeines Sturmabzeichen*)

Designed by the Berlin firm of Wilhelm Ernst Peekhaus on the instructions of the *Oberkommando des Heeres*, this badge was approved by Generaloberst von Brauchitsch on 1 June 1940. It was intended for award to those troops involved in combat actions who, not being infantry *per se*, did not qualify for the Infantry Assault Badge. This covered such troops as artillery, pioneers, tank destroyers, etc. Medical personnel serving in combat conditions were also eligible. In order to qualify for the badge, recipients had to have taken part in at least three separate assault actions on three separate occasions.

The badge consists of a vertical oval wreath of oakleaves in the centre of which is a stylized Wehrmacht eagle clutching a swastika in its talons. The eagle sits upon a crossed stick grenade and bayonet. On the reverse is a hinged pin fitting though screwback fittings are also known. The finish of the badge ranges from silver plate to dull zinc. The award came from the manufacturer in a protective envelope and was accompanied by a certificate of entitlement. An entry was also made in the soldier's paybook.

As the war progressed it became clear that the basic badge for three engagements had become inadequate, many soldiers having taken part in scores of actions. Four additional badges were instituted on 22 June 1943 to indicate participation in 25, 50, 75 and 100 engagements with the enemy.

The 25/50 pattern was similar to the basic pattern but slightly larger and had the central eagle and crossed grenade and bayonet motif struck as a separate piece and affixed to the wreath by four small rivets. The wreath was finished in a matt silver colour, while the central motif was in a dark gunmetal colour. At the base was a small rectangular box bearing the numerals 25 or 50. The 75/100 pattern badge was significantly larger and had the wreath finished in a matt gilt colour. The eagle was also correspondingly larger. At the base was a box bearing the numerals 75 or 100.

Credit for the award of the new grades could be back-dated to the date of the invasion of the Soviet Union. Those with eight months' combat service were credited with 10 actions, those with twelve months' service 15 actions and those with fifteen months' service 25 actions. Thus it can be seen that, for example, an assault pioneer having served continuously in a combat role on the Eastern Front since the invasion would immediately qualify for the 25 pattern badge on its institution. These numbered badges are very rare, and very high-quality reproductions which are extremely difficult to detect are now circulating.

The basic General Assault Badge can be clearly seen in the photographs of Wilhelm Wegener and Wolfgang von Bostell.

The Close Combat Clasp (*Nahkampfspange*)

By 1942 it had become clear that the Infantry Assault Badge was woefully inadequate to reward the continued efforts of Germany's infantrymen and on 25 November 1942 a new award, the Close Combat Clasp, was instituted. This consists of a horizontal spray of oakleaves having in its centre a square section bearing an eagle and swastika with outspread wings, over a crossed stick grenade and bayonet. This central section was pierced out and a small gunmetal coloured metal plate fitted to the reverse to help highlight the design. The badge was die struck in zinc and appropriately finished in bronze, silver or gilt. It featured a wide flat horizontal pin fitting and was worn above the left breast pocket.

The badge was awarded in three grades:

First Grade – bronze	awarded for 15 days' close-quarter fighting
Second Grade – silver	awarded for 30 days' close-quarter fighting
Third Grade – gold	awarded for 50 days' close-quarter fighting

If the soldier were wounded in action, the criteria were reduced to 10, 20 and 40 days respectively. In view of the fact that the award could be back-dated, a scale of combat days to length of service was devised giving five days' credit for 8 months' service, ten days for 12 months' service and fifteen days' for 15 months' service. The length of service had to be spent in continuous fighting.

Hitler made it quite clear that he regarded the Close Combat Clasp in Gold to be an exceptionally high decoration and reserved the right to award it personally, each recipient receiving a special 21-days' leave. It was regarded as almost as high an award as the Knight's Cross. It was, in fact, more rare; by the end of the war only 403 awards of the Close Combat Clasp in Gold had been made.

Whereas most of these clasps were awarded in cellophane packets which were quickly discarded, the Gold grade came in a high-quality black case lined with velvet, a further indicator of its high status. In fact, each recipient received two Gold Badges. One was identical in manufacture with the bronze and silver grades and came in a cellophane packet. This was for everyday wear on the combat tunic. The second piece, in its fitted, velvet-lined case, had a superior quality matt gilt finish with burnished highlights. Instead of the metal backing plate being attached by merely crimping it to the reverse, it was neatly riveted in place. At the top reverse there was also a small hook just behind the eagle the more securely to affix the badge to the tunic. In conjunction with the award came a certificate of entitlement. An entry of the award would be made in the soldier's paybook as well as a record of the combat days for which the award had been earned.

The Close Combat Clasp, in its bronze grade, can be clearly seen in the photograph of Franz Weber.

The Tank Destruction Badge (*Panzervernichtungsabzeichen*)

The full title of this badge – *Sonderabzeichen für das Niederkämpfen von Panzerkampfwagen durch Einzelkämpfer* (Special Badge for Single-Handed Destruction of a Tank) – explains its purpose well. It was for award to any individual soldier who through his own sole actions destroyed an enemy tank using hand-held weapons such as grenades, magnetic mines, satchel charges, Panzerfaust, etc. Anti-tank gunners for example would not qualify, as the entire gun crew would be considered responsible for the victory and not one individual soldier.

Many courageous infantrymen and grenadiers calmly lay in their foxholes as enemy tanks rolled over them, only to leap out and plant their charges on the thinly armoured engine deck or turret overhang and disable or destroy the enemy. This highly esteemed award was instituted on 9 March 1942, and awards could be back-dated to 21 June 1941, the date of the invasion of the Soviet Union.

The award consisted of a 90mm-long piece of braid, 32mm wide with black borders, on to which was pinned a thin, stamped metal stylized tank motif. Reinforced by a metal backing plate, the award was sewn to the upper right sleeve of the tunic. Initially the braid was in aluminium thread and one was given for each tank destroyed. On 18 December 1943, the *Oberkommando des Heeres* authorized a further grade in gold braid to recognize the destruction of five enemy tanks, both grades being worn in conjunction with each other as appropriate. For example, a soldier decorated for destroying seven enemy tanks would wear one gold and two silver awards. The gold badge would be worn above the two silver. The maximum known to have been awarded was twenty-one (four gold and one silver). This amazing achievement was by Knight's Cross winner Oberstleutnant Günter Viezenz of Grenadier Regiment 7.

There appears to have been confusion over the colour of the tank used for each type of braid. On the standard aluminium braid award, the tank is in gun-metal colour. On the gold braid type, however, tanks in gold, silver and gun-metal are known. The badge was accompanied by a certificate of entitlement and an entry made in the soldier's paybook. When the gold award was presented, the preceding four silver awards had to be returned.

A similar badge for the shooting down of an enemy aircraft by small-arms fire was also approved. In the centre was a representation of an aircraft in place of the tank. It is unlikely that any of these were actually manufactured as no original examples with guaranteed provenance have ever appeared.

Panzer Assault Badge in Bronze
(*Panzerkampfabzeichen in Bronze*)

Instituted on 1 June 1940, the bronze version of the Panzer Assault Badge was issued to panzer grenadier personnel, i.e., armoured infantry who travelled in half-tracked armoured personnel carriers, etc., as opposed to motorized infantry – those who travelled in lorries, who received the bronze version of the Infantry Assault Badge.

The badge consists of a vertical oval of oakleaves with a closed-winged Wehrmacht eagle at its top. Within the wreath is a stylized representation of a Panzerkampfwagen Mk IV facing right. On the reverse is a hinged vertical pin fitting for attaching the badge to the left breast pocket of the tunic. In June 1943, special versions were instituted to acknowledge participation in 25, 50, 75 and 100 actions. The 25/50 version is slightly larger than the basic badge and has the tank separately affixed by rivets. The 75/100 version is larger still and features a gilt tank on a bronze wreath. These numbered versions are extremely rare and are now being expertly reproduced.

The basic version of the Panzer Assault Badge in bronze can be clearly seen in the photograph of Georg Karck.

Luftwaffe Ground Combat Badge
(*Erdkampfabzeichen der Luftwaffe*)

This badge was instituted on 31 March 1942 by Reichsmarschall Hermann Göring. It was designed by Professor von Weech and comprises a vertical oval wreath of oakleaves topped by the distinctive Luftwaffe-style flying eagle with a swastika in its talons. In the centre is an ominous-looking thundercloud from which a large lightning bolt strikes the ground below. The wreath and eagle were silvered and the central design chemically blackened, or, in late war versions, painted.

The badge measures 56mm × 43mm and has a vertical hinged pin on the reverse for attaching to the tunic. Badges were initially struck in tombakbronze (pinchback) but this was later changed to zinc. The earliest pieces were of the finest quality, having a separately struck eagle attached to the badge with two or three rivets. The pin was wide and flattened, as on many of the better quality decorations. As time progressed and manufacture was simplified, one rivet was used, then the badge was finally cast in one piece. The pin was now simply formed from a piece of thin wire stock. Embroidered cloth versions in coloured threads and wire were also produced but their extreme rarity suggests that they were not often worn.

This badge was intended as an award for those Luftwaffe soldiers serving in such units as the Luftwaffe Feld Divisionen, the Hermann Göring Division, etc., as well as to paratroopers, who, later in the war, were as often as not deployed in an infantry role, and never qualified for their Paratrooper Badge. This badge then, could be considered as a direct equivalent to the Infantry Assault Badge. Its award criteria were almost identical, requiring the participation of the recipient in three specific individual assaults on three separate occasions.

Any Luftwaffe soldier who had previously qualified for the Army's Infantry Assault Badge could exchange it for the Ground Combat Badge, and any Luftwaffe soldier killed during the course of a ground assault automatically qualified posthumously for the award.

The badge was initially supplied in a box with the title *Erdkampf-Abzeichen* embossed in gilt gothic letters on the lid, though latterly a simple paper packet was used. It was accompanied by an award certificate; some of these were large and elaborate, others were simply typewritten slips of paper.

As the war progressed, variants of the badge were produced. Instituted on 10 November 1944, these were of almost identical design, but were slightly larger and featured a plaque at the base bearing the numeral 25, 50, 75 or 100 to signify the number of ground assaults in which the recipient had participated. While these badges appear to have been manufactured, there seems to be no evidence that any were actually awarded. It may well be that awards on paper were made instead, because apparently original examples of the basic badge exist which seem to have been field modified by the addition of the numbered plaque, presumably because of a lack of supplies of the real thing.

Original examples of the numbered badges are exceedingly rare, and many of those that appear in collections are in fact genuine post-war de-nazified West German versions of the badge which have been altered by the addition of a wartime eagle and swastika badge. As many of the post-war pieces date from as early as 1957, they have considerable age patina and may appear quite genuine, especially as some used original wartime stocks of pins and hinges, etc.

The Ground Combat Badge of the Luftwaffe can be seen worn next to the Iron Cross on the breast pocket of Siegfried Jamrowski.

Luftwaffe Close Combat Clasp (*Nahkampfspange der Luftwaffe*)

Instituted on 3 November 1944, this clasp was intended to reward the gallantry of Luftwaffe soldiers engaged in hand-to-hand combat.

The badge took the form of a circular laurel wreath with a spray of oakleaves at each side, identical in design with the range of flight clasps produced for the Luftwaffe's flight personnel. In the centre was a Luftwaffe-style flying eagle clutching a swastika in its talons, over a crossed stick-grenade and bayonet. The clasp was to be worn on the left breast pocket.

The clasp was instituted in three grades:

First Grade – bronze for 15 days' close-quarter fighting

Second Grade – silver for 30 days' close-quarter fighting

Third Grade – gold for 50 days' close-quarter fighting

Awards of this badge 'on paper' were certainly made on a number of occasions and it is thought that some actual examples of the bronze clasp may have been issued, although no photographic evidence of this has yet appeared. Little if any evidence of the award of the silver or gold grade clasps has come to light. Some sources quote awards of the gold grade in January 1945, but it may well be that it was the standard Army pattern Close Combat Clasp which was actually presented, as had been the usual practice until then. As with the Army clasp, recipients of the Luftwaffe's gold grade were to receive a special 21-days' leave.

Parachutist Badge (*Fallschirmschützenabzeichen*)

Not an infantry badge *per se*, but as the paratroops were increasingly used as ground infantry in the latter part of the war, this badge came to be worn by many soldiers fighting in an infantry role.

It was in fact a qualification badge, awarded to paratroopers who had satisfactorily carried out the required training, including six jumps. The badge was instituted on 5 November 1936 and consists of an oval wreath with oakleaves to the right and laurel to the left. In the centre is a large, diving eagle clutching a swastika in its talons. The eagle is in a gilt finish while the wreath is in silver which was often chemically darkened. Material ranged from plated bronze to aluminium or zinc.

On the reverse is a vertical hinged pin fitting. Embroidered versions in cotton thread for other ranks and wire embroidery for officers were also produced.

The badge was awarded with a certificate of entitlement and was issued in a square box in dark blue with the title of the award embossed in gilt gothic characters on the lid. The lid interior was blue silk, the base was blue velvet or flock.

The Parachutist Badge can be seen, in its metal form, in the photograph of Bruno Sassen, and in its wire embroidered form, in the photograph of Heinrich Neumann.

⚔ The German Cross

This impressive decoration was introduced on 28 September 1941. Designed by Professor Klein of Munich, on Hitler's direction, it was intended to recognize acts of gallantry or meritorious service which were greater than that required to attract the Iron Cross First Class but which would not merit the Knight's Cross. Although this award fell somewhere between the First Class Iron Cross and the Knight's Cross it was not part of the Iron Cross series, but an entirely independent award. Many soldiers were awarded the German Cross after the Knight's Cross had been won, something which would not have happened had the German Cross been part of the Iron Cross series.

The award consisted of a large silver sunburst star approximately 63mm in diameter. Superimposed upon this was a smaller star of identical design, but in a dark gunmetal colour, thus giving the impression of a dark sunburst with a silver edge. In the middle was a matt silver disc in the centre of which sat a large black enamelled swastika (the 'German' cross of the title). Surrounding this centrepiece was a wreath of laurel leaves with the date of institution, 1941, at its base. On the reverse was a large flat hinged pin used to attach the award to the right breast pocket of the tunic. The complex multi-part construction was held together with either four or six rivets depending on the manufacturer.

The award came in two types: a silver grade for military service and a gold grade for gallantry or outstanding achievements in combat. Only the colour of the laurel wreath altered. With it came a certificate of possession and on occasions an impressive citation, and was presented in a black case, the base of which was covered with black velvet and the lid with white silk.

Because of its rather complex construction, it was fairly heavy and unwieldy to wear, so a special version in cloth embroidery was also manufactured. This, apart from the laurel wreath which was the same metal component as used in the standard badge, was entirely embroidered in appropriately coloured threads upon a cloth backing of the same colour as the wearer's uniform, i.e., field grey for the army, blue-grey for the Luftwaffe, etc.

Approximately 30,000 German Crosses in gold were awarded, of which some 17,000 went to the army and Waffen-SS.

A special grade in gold which had the laurel wreath studded with small diamonds was manufactured by the firm of Rath in Munich. None of these was ever awarded and the criteria for their award is unknown.

As a result of their popularity on the collectors' market, these awards have been widely reproduced. Although earlier copies lacked the quality of manufacture of the originals, the most recent have been almost perfect, and collectors should exercise extreme caution.

The Iron Cross

All the soldiers featured in this book won both the Iron Cross Second Class and First Class.

The Second Class was worn only on the day of the award, pinned to the tunic or with the ribbon tucked into the tunic buttonhole. Subsequently, only the ribbon was worn, sewn diagonally into the second buttonhole of the tunic. See the photograph of Franz Weber for a clear view of this buttonhole arrangement. The Iron Cross Second Class came wrapped in tissue in a paper envelope which was usually discarded. As an alternative to the buttonhole arrangement, the Iron Cross ribbon could be worn on a ribbon bar above the breast pocket. See the photograph of Wilhelm Wegener for an example of this.

The Iron Cross Second Class measured about 43mm and consisted of a black iron centre held within a silvered frame with a loop on the upper rim to accept the ribbon. This ring occasionally can be found to carry a manufacturer's code number. More than 2 million awards were made.

The Iron Cross First Class, identical in design with the Second Class, featured instead of a ribbon, a plain reverse with a hinged pin fitting used to attach the Cross to the left breast pocket of the tunic. It can be seen thus in many of the photographs in this book. Occasional examples may be encountered with a screwback rather than a pin fitting. These were privately purchased by the recipients.

The Iron Cross First Class came in a black case bearing the outline of the Cross impressed in silver on the lid. The base was covered with white velvet or flock and the lid was lined with white satin. Approximately 300,000 were awarded.

The Knight's Cross

The Knight's Cross of the Iron Cross was a newcomer, added to the Iron Cross series in September 1939 to bridge the considerable gap which existed between the Iron Cross First Class and the Grand Cross of the Iron Cross. Up until 1918, this gap had been filled by the Prussian *Pour-le-Mérite*, the famous 'Blue Max', but this was no longer available so a new decoration was instituted – the Knight's Cross.

The Knight's Cross consisted of a blackened iron centre contained within a genuine silver frame. The obverse featured in the centre a swastika and in the lower arm the year of institution, 1939. On the reverse was only the date of the original institution, 1813, in the lower arm. The silver frame had an inner beaded rim which was usually finished in an attractive matt silver oxide effect with a plain, highly polished outer rim. At the top of the rim to the upper arm was a small eyelet through which the loop for the neck ribbon passed. The reverse upper rim, just below the eyelet, usually carried the silver content code '800' with the manufacturer's code number where applicable. Only three firms manufactured this award officially: Steinhauer und Lück of Ludenscheid, Deschler of Munich and C. E. Junker of Berlin. Others are known to have made the Knight's Cross but did so unofficially and against regulations. The manufacturers' codes which can be found on those Knight's Crosses produced by the official manufacturers were: '4' for Steinhauer und Lück (although their Crosses are generally unmarked), '1' for Deschler and L/12 for Junker.

The Knight's Cross measured about 48mm and was worn suspended from the neck by a 45mm-wide ribbon. This ribbon was used on the actual award day, but afterwards the recipient could use any method of attaching he desired. This usually took the form of a short piece of ribbon for the area that could be seen at the front of the collar, with tie strings of ribbon, cord or even elastic securing the cross underneath the collar. Examination of the photograph of Georg Karck will show that he has used a metal chain to suspend his Knight's Cross.

The Knight's Cross was awarded with a rectangular black case the fitted base of which was covered with black velvet and the lid lined with white satin.

It was not unknown for the *Ritterkreuzträger* to wear a modified Iron Cross Second Class at the neck when in combat rather than risk damage or loss of the true Knight's Cross. Additionally, especially late in the war, supplies of the Knight's Cross were not always available at the front, and the recipient may have had no option but to accept the Second Class as a temporary substitute. The author knows of at least one *Ritterkreuzträger*, who, anticipating that his awards would be looted at the end of the war, sent his Ritterkreuz home a short time before the capitulation, substituting it with a Second Class. True enough, his Soviet captors immediately stole all his awards, but his *Ritterkreuz* was safe at home. He retains it in his possession to this day.

At the end of the war the situation was so chaotic that some soldiers nominated for the Knight's Cross had the awards approved, but were never informed of the fact. As late as the seventies, soldiers were still being informed that they had in fact been awarded the Knight's Cross in the last few days of the war. In addition, many soldiers purchased additional spare Knight's Crosses from approved uniform outfitters. These could range from pieces with plated zinc or brass rims, to those with rims having a silver content higher than that of the award piece, depending on how much the soldier wished to pay.

A total of something in excess of 7,000 Knight's Crosses were awarded. Unfortunately their rarity and high value today has led to them being widely reproduced. These copies range from crude one-piece lead castings through to high quality three-part die strikings manufactured in exactly the same manner as the originals. Many of these latter pieces bear the L/12 mark.

The Oakleaves

The Oakleaves were instituted on 3 June 1940 to recognize the performance of additional acts of gallantry or meritorious conduct in combat after the Knight's Cross had been won.

The Oakleaves consisted of a spray of three leaves with the central leaf superimposed over the outer two. The piece was die-struck in solid silver with a plain, slightly concave finish to the reverse. Attached to the reverse was a replacement ribbon loop. The obverse was finished in a matt silver oxide effect with the highlights burnished. Presented in a black case with a replacement length of neck ribbon, the Oakleaves were simply clipped to the eyelet on the Knight's Cross in place of the original ribbon loop.

Some 883 awards of the Oakleaves were made. Originals are very rare and fetch high prices.

The photograph of Wolfgang von Bostell shows the standard award Oakleaves being worn, while those worn by Heinrich Keese are in fact a replica set made in the field by his men as a token of esteem, cut from hammered down silver coins.

The Swords and Oakleaves, Swords Oakleaves and Diamonds, and Golden Swords Oakleaves and Diamonds are not described here as none of the soldiers featured in this book bore these decorations.

THE MEN

1939–40

The first Knight's Crosses were awarded in late September 1939. From then until the end of the year the vast majority of awards were to generals and other senior ranking officers for their successful command of their troops during the Polish Campaign. During the Western Campaign of 1940, however, some Knight's Crosses were awarded to individual soldiers for acts of gallantry.

As well as a number of awards to Luftwaffe aces for achieving considerable scores of enemy pilots downed, the first examples of exceptional daring and *élan* such as the capture of the Belgian forts at Eben Emael – which were to be but a taste of things to come as far as German feats of arms were concerned – brought about several well-earned awards to soldiers who had shown exceptional courage and determination in battle against vastly superior enemy forces. The Western Campaign was short, however, and the rapidity of the German victory meant that the opportunities for the soldier to show his prowess and gallantry in action were short-lived. Of course the airman and sailor continued to see action during this period, but for the infantryman, there ensued a period of well-earned rest.

As far as the first year of the war is concerned then, most awards were for leadership or for proficiency in action, and mostly to senior officers. The day of the common footsoldier was yet to come. From the start of the war until the end of 1940, fewer than 450 Knight's Crosses had been awarded. The majority of these, some 300 or so, were awarded during the campaign in France and the Low Countries.

The Knight's Cross of the Iron Cross was still a rarely seen decoration, worn by only a tiny fraction of one per cent of the men under arms. By the end of hostilities some 7,000 soldiers bore this most distinctive and prestigious symbol in recognition of their deeds by a grateful nation.

Major Georg Michael

Georg Michael was born in Hamburg on 10 December 1917, the son of a Naval Officer. After completing his compulsory spell of duty with the

Reichsarbeitsdienst, he commenced military service with Kavallerie Regiment 13 in Lüneburg. By the outbreak of war in September 1939, Michael had reached the rank of Wachtmeister and during the Polish Campaign he served as a section leader in 6 Squadron of Kavallerie Regiment 22.

On 1 March 1940, Michael was commissioned Leutnant and subsequently gained much valuable combat experience during the early part of the invasion of France where he showed considerable determination in the attack and was decorated with the Iron Cross Second Class on 25 May, and the First Class on 27 June. He also qualified for his Infantry Assault Badge.

At the end of June Michael found himself leading a reconnaissance mission into enemy territory. Only six other mounted soldiers accompanied him, plus a motorcycle dispatch rider. The small group of cavalrymen encountered a pair of French stragglers and stopped to radio back a report to Regimental HQ. Slightly irritated at the delay, Michael dismounted from his own horse and decided to proceed as pillion rider on the dispatch-rider's motor cycle. The initial objective was the small village of Fremontier la Petite. No one was sure whether the village was occupied by the enemy or not. It should have been clear but the situation was by no means certain. Reaching the village, Michael and his motor cyclist found four French pioneers ensconced there, but they quickly gave themselves up, having no stomach for a fight. Then the sound of engine noises came from an easterly direction. No German units were expected – they could only be enemy. Luckily, for them, only one vehicle appeared, a jeep containing a French major and his adjutant. They too were quickly overpowered and taken prisoner.

Meanwhile, the village had been checked and secured. The patrol had already taken a number of prisoners including a senior officer. Michael however, decided to proceed further, past the village and check the route for road blocks, mines, etc. At the same time, he radioed back to the spearhead unit of the division, that the village was clear of enemy forces.

On the east edge of the village, the dispatch rider was standing sentry. Suddenly, a message came back from him that enemy forces could be seen only a kilometre or two distant, approaching the village in some strength. Michael was stunned. He had already reported the village clear and the spearhead unit was approaching fast. Now it looked as if this sizeable French force might encircle the village and capture both Michael and his reconnaissance troop as well as the regimental spearhead.

Michael had no time to consider his situation. Immediate action was required and he immediately jumped on to the motor cycle, the dispatch-rider taking the jeep and following directly behind him. At full speed they shot along the small road leading out of the village and through a small wood towards the enemy. Turning a bend in the road, Michael found himself slap in the middle of a company of coloured Senegalese troops, commanded by French officers. The French immediately opened fire. Michael's reactions were fast however as he threw himself from the motor cycle into a roadside ditch. Thinking fast, he yelled to the French troops not to fire, he had come to negotiate. The Senegalese soldiers obeyed as one of the French officers walked over and asked Michael how he had come by the Battalion Commander's jeep.

The quick thinking and cool-headed Michael quickly responded that the Germans were holding the French major hostage and that he had been sent to negotiate terms for the honourable surrender of the French. Pointing in the direction of the village, Michael told the French officer that the German artillery was positioned there and in twenty-five minutes would begin a bombardment. The French must quickly decide whether to surrender or not. Now the senior French officer appeared. His face a mask of fury, he asked how dare the impertinent German demand surrender, it was he who was the prisoner.

Michael's bluff appeared to have failed, but he was unwilling to give up so easily. He was a proud member of an élite cavalry unit and would not countenance defeat. Now his strength of character and determination came to the fore. Outwardly calm, Michael proceeded to warn the French officer of the horrible consequences of a refusal to surrender. He could see that the Frenchman's determination was wavering. His bluff might yet work.

Maintaining his outwardly calm appearance, he demanded to know if the French really wanted useless bloodshed. Behind him, he said, was a battle-hardened cavalry division whose regiments even now were manoeuvring to surround the French, – they would be annihilated. In a loud voice he asked 'Where is your authority for this sacrifice?' On a map he indicated his regimental and Abteilung HQ positions and insisted that an honourable surrender would be no disgrace. 'Lay down your arms and surrender. You will be well treated. The officers can keep their swords and horses. The wounded will be taken to hospital in Chartres for treatment and a certificate will be issued to confirm that you only surrendered to save unnecessary bloodshed when faced by an overwhelmingly superior force, this will protect you in any potential court martial.'

Leutnant Michael allowed the French some time to consider. There were certainly disagreements. The younger officers foolhardily wished to fight on, and break out of the German encirclement. The older officers, completely taken in by Michael's act and his calm confident manner, were less rash. Convinced that a large German force awaited them, and well aware that their colonial troops were by no means an élite force, their opinion won through. The French force surrendered to Michael and marched off into captivity. Some 500 enemy prisoners were thus taken by just two German soldiers.

Michael's regiment was astounded when they heard of his sheer audacity. In the face of such a huge force of enemy troops, Michael had not only not surrendered, but by sheer audacity and barefaced cheek, persuaded *them* to surrender to *him*. Not only had some 500 prisoners been taken, but a major battle had been averted which would almost certainly have cost many lives. Michael's exploits were mentioned in the official Armed Forces Dispatches and his grateful regiment recommended him for the Knight's Cross of the Iron Cross. This was finally approved and awarded on 19 January 1941. On 1 February he was promoted to Oberleutnant.

In the summer of 1941, Oberleutnant Michael led 6 Squadron, Kavallerie Regiment 22 in the 1 Kavallerie Division. It fought very well at the crossing of the Dnieper and at Smolensk. During the retreat through the Pripet marshes it was used to protect the southern flank of Guderian's Second Panzerarmee, acquitting itself well before being withdrawn from the front to France where it was refitted and upgraded to an armoured unit, being retitled 24th Panzer Division. Kavallerie Regiment 22 became Panzer Grenadier Regiment 26, Michael still serving with 6 Kompanie.

On its return to the front, the division was attached to Sixth Army in the drive to Stalingrad, and with the bulk of the army the division was virtually annihilated in this battle, Michael himself being severely wounded. Once again duing the hectic fighting throughout the terrible Russian winter, Michael showed such determination and total disregard for his own safety in numerous actions that he was recommended for the Oakleaves by his Divisional Commander. On 25 January 1943 a telegram arrived from Führer Headquarters addressed to Michael. It read 'In grateful appreciation of your heroic actions in battle, for the future of our people, I award you, as the 187th soldier of the German Wehrmacht, the Oakleaves to the Knight's Cross of the Iron Cross. Adolf Hitler.'

In March–April of 1943, the divisional remnant moved back to France where the unit was rebuilt, being sent briefly to Italy before returning to the Eastern Front just in time for yet another horrific Russian winter. It fought in the battle for Kiev in November, suffering terrible casualties. During February 1944, the division took part in the relief of the encircled German units at Cherkassy, serving with such distinction that the entire division was mentioned in dispatches. During the spring it was again brutally mauled by overwhelming

Russian forces during the retreat from the Dnieper. On 17 January 1944, in bitter fighting in the area around Nikopol on the southern sector of the Eastern Front, Michael was wounded in action for the eighth time. The wound proved fatal and this brave man succumbed on 18 January 1944.

Major Rudolf Witzig

Rudolf Witzig was born in Röhlinghausen on 14 August 1916. At the age of 19 he commenced his military career when in April 1935, he joined the army's Pioniere Bataillon 16 in Höxter as an officer cadet. His basic military training completed, he attended the Kriegsschule in Dresden and the Pionierschule in Rehagen-Klausdorf, being commissioned Leutnant in April 1937. He was then posted as a Platoon Commander to Pioniere Bataillon 31 where he served for some ten months before volunteering for paratroop training and was in August 1938 posted to the Pioniere Zug of the Fallschirm Infanterie Bataillon in Brunswick. Two months later Witzig had completed his parachute training and on 1 October 1938 he qualified for the Paratrooper Badge of the Army.

The Commander-in-Chief of the Luftwaffe, however, had cast his covetous eye on the paratroopers and persuaded Hitler that, as they were essentially airborne, they should belong to the Luftwaffe. Hitler agreed, though he did insist that once they had landed they were then ground troops and would come under command of the army senior command on that sector of the front. Like all the army's paratroops, Witzig found himself transferred to the Luftwaffe in December 1938. In July 1939 he was promoted to Oberleutnant. At the end of October Witzig was given command of the Pioniere Zug of Fallschirmjäger Sturm Abteilung 'Koch' and subsequently, on 1 April 1940, 17 Kompanie, Fallschirmjäger Regiment 1.

On 9 April 1940, Germany launched the invasion of Norway and Denmark. The Fallschirmjäger participated in both actions and, particularly in Norway, served with great distinction, proving themselves tough and resilient troops. It was, however, during the opening phase of the campaign in the West that the Fallschirmjäger were to achieve one of the great victories of the war.

Hitler had decided that the Fallschirmjäger were to be dropped ahead of the main assault to seize key bridges and installations. On the Belgian frontier sat the newly constructed fortress of Eben Emael in a commanding position to protect the Albert Canal. With some eighteen artillery pieces in concrete emplacements six feet thick plus numerous machine-gun and anti-tank positions, the fort was built into the wall of the Canal itself and could prove a formidable obstacle to the German advance.

An audacious plan was drawn up by General Student, the commander of the Luftwaffe's parachute troops, whereby a special combat assault group commanded by Hauptmann Köch would assault the fort and the bridges at Veldvezelt, Vroenhoven and Canne. The assault on the fort itself would be carried out by the Pioniere Kompanie of II Bataillon, Fallschirmjäger Regiment 1 under the command of Oberleutnant Witzig.

At just over 0500 on 10 May 1940, Witzig and his men were above the fort aboard DFS230 Gliders. Unfortunately, Witzig's own landing had to be aborted due to a problem with the glider and he had to return to base to pick up a new DFS230. The remainder of his group landed on top of the Eben Emael fort, stunning the Belgian defenders. Leaping from the gliders even as they touched down, the Fallschirmjäger, under the command of Oberfeldwebel Wenzel, stormed into the defenders with flame-throwers, grenades and explosive charges specially designed to destroy the concrete casemates of the fort. So ferocious was the attack, that within just a few minutes fourteen guns had been destroyed and the exit doors of the fort blown open. The Germans had forced entry into the fort, but the remainder of the complex was still in Belgian hands and the garrison troops now began to rally and fight back. The Belgians called down artillery fire on their own positions, hoping to wipe out the Fallschirmjäger on the roof of the fort.

Some three hours later, Witzig finally reached the fort in his glider, to find that his men had been pinned down by the enemy artillery, and were sheltering in the captured casemates. Forced to shelter there for the night, the small group of Fallschirmjäger were reinforced by more Fallschirmjäger when morning broke. Bolstered by this reinforcement, Witzig rallied his men to one great effort and at the head of his small force, led them into the attack. The ferocious new assault disheartened the beseiged garrison, who decided to hoist the white flag and surrender. Witzig and his 85-strong assault group had defeated a powerful modern fortress garrisoned by more than 1,200 men. Only six of Witzig's men had been lost. This was a superb tactical victory for Germany as well as being a tremendous propaganda coup.

On 11 May 1940, a special Wehrmacht Communiqué was released. 'The powerful fortress of Eben Emael, commanding the crossings of the Maas and the Albert Canal was taken on Saturday evening. The Commandant and his 1,000 men were taken prisoner. The Fort was on 10 May put out of action by a hand-picked detachment of Luftwaffe personnel under the command of Oberleutnant Witzig, using new combat methods, and the garrison captured. Following the arrival of units of the army after hard fighting from the north to join up with Witzig's detachment, the enemy laid down their arms.'

Oberleutnant Witzig was immediately recommended for the

Knight's Cross of the Iron Cross which Hitler quickly approved. Witzig was awarded the Knight's Cross with an effective date of 10 May. He had not yet won the Iron Cross in Second or First Classes, however, and these were a requisite for the award of the Knight's Cross. The two lower grades therefore were also quickly approved, but dated as 12 May for the Second Class and 13 May for the First Class. Witzig and his men were moved into Maastricht after the victorious action for well-earned food and an equally appreciated chance to sleep. A stream of dignitaries then arrived, wishing to congratulate the hardy paras, General Student, Reichsmarschall Göring and Hitler himself all arrived to greet the heroes of Eben Emael. Every soldier who took part was decorated and promoted one rank. Witzig therefore attained the rank of Hauptmann with immediate effect.

For the next two months Witzig was attached to the Command Staff of the Air Ministry in Berlin, serving as an adjutant to Göring. The Reichsmarschall delighted in basking in the reflected glory of his young Fallschirmjäger heroes.

On 1 August 1940, Hauptmann Witzig was posted to take command of 9 Kompanie, Fallschirmjäger Sturm Regiment 1 and took part in the attack on Crete, being wounded in action in combat near Maleme airfield. He was evacuated to the Luftwaffe hospital in Athens before returning to Germany for further treatment. In spring 1942, he took command of the Fallschirm Korps Pioniere Bataillon, serving in Tunisia, seeing action almost immediately on arrival at the defence of Djebel Abiod. Just over a week later, he was in command of a Kampfgruppe which included a Panzer Kompanie, 3 Fallschirmjäger Kompanie, as well as artillery, Flak and anti-tank support. Witzig and his Kampfgruppe repulsed a British attack along the coastal road. By now holding the rank of major, Witzig was awarded the Kreta Cuffband for his part in the Crete battle in November 1942, shortly after this new award was instituted.

On 26 February 1943 Witzig's force successfully attacked the British positions in the hills north of Sedjenane and expelled the enemy, pursuing them through the village and engaging in bitter hand-to-hand combat with the retreating British. As the campaign in North Africa drew to a close, Major Witzig was one of a small group of officers who escaped capture by crossing to Sicily in a small motor boat. On 1 May 1943, Witzig was awarded the Afrika commemorative Cuffband.

June of 1944 found Witzig in command of I Bataillon, Fallschirm Pionier Regiment 21, preparing for action on the Eastern Front. Committed to battle in July, it fought as part of Kampfgruppe Schirmer. On 25 July the regiment set off on a long forced march along the route from Kowno–Dünaburg, reaching by that evening the village of Jonava.

On 26 July the enemy attacked with strong armoured support. Witzig and his men rose to the challenge, however, and within a very short time had destroyed some fifteen enemy tanks with bazookas and Panzerfausts. A special supplement to the Wehrmacht dispatches reported: 'In the battlefield west of Kauen the I Bataillon of Fallschirm Pionier Regiment 21 under the command of Major Witzig, through exemplary combat spirit proved itself outstanding. The Bataillon, on this day, destroyed 27 enemy tanks in close-quarter battle.' Witzig then gathered his depleted forces and led a successful forced march westwards to safety, avoiding certain encirclement and captivity. Witzig had once again shown great gallantry in action against overwhelming enemy forces and had set a shining example to his men, inspiring them to superhuman efforts. He was awarded the Oakleaves to his Knight's Cross on 25 November 1944, the 662nd recipient of this high award.

In December 1944, Major Witzig took command of Fallschirm-jäger Regiment 18, in 6 Fallschirm Division, seeing further action in Holland and the Rhineland, doggedly resisting the advance of the Western Allies before finally surrendering in May 1945. As a final honour, during this month, Witzig's name was added to the Roll of Honour of the German Air Force. He remained in captivity for just four months before being released.

This, however, was by no means the end of this brave soldier's military career. In January 1956 he joined the Federal West German Army, the Bundesheer, with the rank of Oberstleutnant and was in command of the Pionier Regiment staff in Düsseldorf. He subsequently commanded Pionier Bataillon 2 and served in the special department for Pionier Weapons and Equipment. In 1965 he joined the Staff of the Pionierschule in Munich and was promoted to Oberst. Rudolf Witzig finally retired in September 1974, having given a total of 28 years of service to his country and received some of its highest decorations in return.

Major Michael Pössinger

Michael Pössinger was born on 18 January 1919 in Ettal in Upper Bavaria, the son of a farmer. From 1925 to 1929 he attended Volkschule in Ettal and from 1929 to 1937 completed his education at the Gymnasium. At the age of 18, Pössinger volunteered for military service and was accepted into 6 Kompanie of 2 Bataillon, Gebirgsjäger Regiment 98 in Lenggries. As a member of 2 Kompanie, Pössinger served as a machine-gunner and took part in the march into Austria where his regiment moved into Innsbruck, and also served during the occupation of the Sudetenland. His military career progressed quite well and by April 1939 he had been promoted to the rank of Unteroffizier. By the outbreak of war, Pössinger was serving as a section leader in an anti-tank platoon of 16 Kompanie of the same Regiment, part of 1 Gebirgs Division which was composed mainly of Bavarians.

The division served on the southern sector of the Polish front, seeing action in the Carpathians where it earned great distinction in the capture of the Dukla Pass near Sanok under command of Generalmajor Kübler. During this action Pössinger was leading a motor-cycle detachment during the assault through the Dukla Pass and into Lemberg, distinguishing himself in action by his cool-headed and determined leadership of his detachment, winning the Iron Cross Second Class.

During the Western Campaign of 1940, the division marched through Luxemburg and Belgium into France, crossing the Maas and seeing action around Fumay, Hurson and the battle for the Aisne–Oise Canal around Caney-le-Château where Pössinger once again distinguished himself by leading his detachment with great *élan* under enemy fire, earning himself the Iron Cross First Class.

His daring in action was further well established on 6 June 1940 during the attack on the Weygand Line at Juvigny where the division was involved in heavy combat against enemy tanks. The division's flanks had come under attack by French armour during an Allied counter-attack. Pössinger and his men immediately went into action, stalking enemy armour with little more than grenades and satchel charges. Within the space of just forty minutes, Pössinger had personally destroyed seven enemy tanks and disabled four more. With such losses the steam quickly ran out of the French attack which rapidly petered out after the loss of its tanks. Pössinger was personally responsible for the blunting of the enemy attack, saving the day for his endangered regiment. With no regard for his own safety he had stalked tank after tank in this most dangerous form of combat. Tank hunting was not for the squeamish and required nerves of steel. His gallantry was rewarded by a recommendation for the Knight's Cross of the Iron Cross and this was personally awarded on 19 July 1940 by his divisional commander Generalmajor Kübler. He was also rewarded with a promotion to Leutnant.

After the successful conclusion of the Western Campaign, the division was moved south into the Balkans in the spring of 1941. It had been earmarked for use in the proposed invasion of Great Britain, Operation 'Sealion', and when this was cancelled, for the proposed capture of Gibraltar. In the event, it served with Second Army during the fight for Yugoslavia, Pössinger being promoted to Oberleutnant during this period.

On the opening of the assault on the Soviet Union, Oberleutnant Pössinger was serving as Company Commander of 6 Kompanie, the unit which he himself had first joined as a private in 1937. The Kompanie served on the south-west sector of the front as part of Heeresgruppe Sud, taking part in the actions at Jazow–Story in June, Winniza in July, Uman–Podwyssokoje in early August and Antonowka in mid September. The battle for the great anti-tank defences at Timoschewka in late September and the attack on Mius–Diakowo in October–November rounded off a very tough and exhausting year of combat for Pössinger and his men. As the unit settled into its winter positions at Mius, Pössinger was tasked to raise a company of ski-troops.

With them, Pössinger spent the first two months of 1942 operating behind enemy lines, attacking supply columns, railway lines and transport trains, and capturing a great deal of weapons and munitions. From divisional intercepts of enemy radio traffic it was learned that the Russians referred to Pössinger's unit as the Ghost Company. Well named, it appeared from nowhere, through the snows, struck and then disappeared as quickly as it had come, operating with minimal losses until a German attack broke through the Russian positions in February and the ski-troops found themselves back with the parent regiment.

By mid May 1942, the division was part of III Panzer Korps and Oberleutnant Pössinger was in command of the spearhead Company of II Bataillon of the regiment during the push towards Kharkov. On the first day, 17 May, Pössinger's company was able to advance through the heavily defended Russian positions and trench systems to a depth of sixteen kilometres. During the attack he was severely wounded and was required to spend two months recuperating in hospital before he could rejoin his unit.

In early September 1942, 1 Gebirgs Division took part in the advance through Dnjepropetrovsk, Tscherkesk-Mikojan-Schachar and the Caucasus in the spearhead of Von Kleist's Caucasus Campaign. As a reinforced Company, Pössinger's unit – part of Kampfgruppe von Hirschfield – took part in the capture of the Kluchar Pass whereby the retreating Russians were cut off and large numbers of prisoners and quantities of matériel were captured.

At the Kluchar Pass, Pössinger was given the order to join a small battle group of three companies and strike south to open the road running to Suchum on the Black Sea, but the Russians were too strong and prevented him from making much progress. The Kampfgruppe was ultimately cut off by the enemy and written off as lost by the Germans. The Russian troops opposing Pössinger were commanded by the man who would eventually become Soviet Defense Minister Gretschkov. Pössinger had lost contact with his own regiment as the pack-mule carrying the radio equipment had been lost. After five days he succeeded in a desperate breakout attempt under cover of darkness, surprising the Soviet troops surrounding him and, after three more days of struggle, reached his own lines. His pleasure in escaping was made even greater when he learned that the enemy propaganda transmissions had already reported the total annihilation of his group several days earlier.

Shortly afterwards the division was located in the Caucasus forests and from there on 13 September 1942 struck through Gunaikaberg, Schaumian–Ssemachoberg on the road towards Tuapse. The Germans renewed the push in the latter part of November, but the steam had run out of their advance. By 24 January 1943, Pössinger's men lay in positions only 150 metres from the enemy positions, but exhausted, could push no further. Now, a Russian counter-attack was to concentrate in pushing the Germans all the way out of the Caucasus, through the Kuban swamps. The division retreated into the Crimea from where it was evacuated to Yugoslavia for rest and refit. During the next few months, while the battered mountain troop division built up its much depleted strength, it saw numerous actions against partisans in Bosnia, Serbia, Montenegro and into Greece.

When, in September 1943, the Italians surrendered to the Allies, the division took part in the disarming of their former Italian comrades in the Anta-Prevesa area. On 23/24 September Pössinger, in command of 6 Kompanie, Gebirgsjäger Regiment 98, took part in the capture of Corfu. More than 4,000 enemy were captured, together with a great quantity of weapons and munitions. Subsequent to this the regiment moved back on to the Greek mainland and undertook further policing actions against partisan units with considerable success. For his command of the company during these anti-partisan battles, Oberleutnant Pössinger was decorated with the German Cross in Gold. In October 1943, he was promoted to Hauptmann and given command of I Bataillon of the regiment which continued to serve in the north of Greece and in Yugoslavia.

In October 1944, Pössinger found himself further promoted, to major, and transferred to take command of II Bataillon, Grenadier Regiment 1128, in the 578th Volks Grenadier Division. This division was serving in East Prussia near Allenstein. Here again, Pössinger's personal gallantry and qualities of leadership came to the fore. In an independent relief attack and breakthrough near Allenstein, he and his men knocked out 42 Russian heavy tanks. Pössinger was recommended for the Oakleaves and on 28 February became the 759th soldier of the Wehrmacht to receive this honour. In February he took command of Grenadier Regiment 1128 and in March was severely wounded for the seventh time. He was evacuated and ultimately reached the hospital in Garmisch where he was taken prisoner by the Americans on 12 May 1945.

After the war, from the summer of 1945 until April 1956 Pössinger became a successful businessman, but in April 1956, as the Federal Republic of Germany began to rebuild its armed forces, Michael Pössinger once more donned the uniform of his country and became a Major, commanding, from July 1956 to October 1961, 104 Gebirgsjäger Bataillon in Mittenwald.

In 1958, Pössinger was promoted to Oberstleutnant. From October 1961 to October 1965, he served as course commander at the Mountain and Winter Warfare School in Mittenwald before, on 1 October 1965, becoming Commander of Defence Command 653. Michael Pössinger retired in 1975 and lives in retirement in Garmisch.

During the war, from 1939 to 1941, Pössinger had been involved with the National Skiing Association and in February 1941 took part in the World Skiing Championship at Cortina d'Ampezzo. After the war he took part in many national and international skiing championships. He was also, between 1948 and 1957 an active bob-sled crewman. Taking part in the 1952 and 1956 Olympics, he was a bronze, silver and gold medallist, as a Bavarian, German and International Champion skier.

SS-Sturmbannführer Fritz Vogt

Fritz Vogt was born on 17 March 1918 in Munich, the son of a Police Leutnant. In 1935, at the age of 17, he volunteered for, and was accepted into the SS-Verfügungstruppe, joining the SS-Standarte Deutschland. After completing his basic military training, he was selected for officer training and was sent to the SS-Junkerschule Braunschweig, being commissioned SS-Untersturmführer on 20 April 1939.

During the Polish Campaign, Vogt served as a platoon commander in a motor cycle unit with such *élan* that he became the first member of the unit to win the Iron Cross Second Class. In 1940, during the Western Campaign, Vogt was a reconnaissance platoon commander with the SS-Verfügungs Division. During the course of the attack on Holland in May 1940, he was located near the border area near Kleve, his recce unit now designated as assault troops for the attack. The Waffen-SS troops were tasked with capturing a bridge on the divsions's line of advance. The approach to the bridge was defended by several bunkers and barricades. Vogt led the attack personally, storming forwards toward the enemy positions and drawing heavy fire upon himself. Miraculously he reached the first of the barricades. One of his NCOs and a machine-gunner arrived hot on his heels, quickly followed by some troops armed with grenade-launchers. Vogt lost no time in continuing his attack and one by one eight enemy bunkers were stormed and eliminated. Astounded by the ferocity of the German attack, the remaining Dutch positions soon gave up. More than 200 Dutch soldiers and their weapons were captured, for the loss of just two German soldiers.

Despite being wounded, Vogt had succeeded in an action of exceptional audacity and determination. From a total of five assault groups which had been assembled for the attack, only Vogt's fully succeeded in meeting the tasks required of them and made the establishment of a bridgehead possible, into which heavy German forces now poured. Already SS-Untersturmführer Vogt was being noticed in the division as a young officer of exceptional ability and undoubted personal gallantry.

On 23 May 1940, Vogt was in Flanders with his now reinforced reconnaissance platoon and was ordered to carry out a reconnaissance in the direction of Aire. Approaching from the south, Vogt spotted a well-equipped French force, in battalion strength, crossing the main road and heading east to attack the advancing Germans. Vogt had no time to deliberate, an immediate decision was required. Undaunted by the enemy strength, Vogt proceeded, with a motor cycle group and two armoured cars, to stalk along the French flanks under cover of a rise in the ground and thick hedging. At almost point-blank range, Vogt's men blasted into the head of the French column, while a light anti-tank gun left behind with the rest of Vogt's small force opened fire at the vehicles at the rear of the French column. Surprise was complete and the demoralized enemy offered virtually no opposition, surrendering quickly. At least 650 heavily armed French soldiers lay down their arms to just thirty SS troopers. Vogt's men suffered no casualties.

By June, Vogt's platoon was south of the Somme. On 7 June they were tasked to carry out yet another reconnaissance from Rouvray-en-Somme towards Harbonnières in the north-west. Near Vrely, Vogt captured two French artillery pieces and surprised a retreating French infantry column, capturing more than 250 prisoners after a short exchange of fire. For his successes in more than twenty reconnaissance missions during the Western Campaign, Vogt was promoted to SS-Obersturmführer and awarded the Iron Cross First Class.

Vogt's personal achievements, however, – more than 1,000 prisoners taken – his audacity and almost reckless personal gallantry in always storming into action at the head of his men oblivious to personal danger, and outstanding leadership, had made it clear to his superiors that something more than an Iron Cross First Class was required sufficiently to reward him. Accordingly, Vogt was recommended for the Knight's Cross of the Iron Cross. This was approved by

Hitler on 4 September 1940, making Vogt only the fifth soldier of the Waffen-SS to be so decorated.

Following the opening of Operation 'Barbarossa', the invasion of the Soviet Union, in June 1941, Vogt had command of 2(Maschinengewehr) Kompanie in the Aufklärungsabteilung of 2nd SS Panzer Grenadier Division Das Reich – the direct descendant of the Verfügungs Division. On 1 July, Vogt received the order to assault the Switocz bridge at Pochowiece as soon as possible and capture it intact, the bridge being essential to the advance of Panzergruppe Guderian.

Vogt's company, reinforced by two large eight-wheeled armoured cars and a self-propelled assault gun set off in the dead of night, using the darkness to cover them on the 27-kilometre journey to the bridge. As he drew near, Vogt decided on a fast surprise assault, splitting his force in two to execute a pincer movement. The first group, led by Oberscharführer Oschner, roared off on their motor cycles, immediately followed by Vogt's second group. Oschner's men sped up the approach road on to the bridge, the grenadiers quickly cutting the fuzes on the demolition charges planted by Russian sappers. The bridge was now intact in German hands, but the Russians had recovered quickly from their surprise and enemy fire now rained down on the small German force. With his two armoured cars and the assault gun, Vogt quickly established a bridgehead on the east bank and quickly organized all-round defence as enemy attacks begun. One enemy armoured vehicle reached within twenty metres of Vogt's positions before being knocked out. Despite many ferocious attacks on the bridge, Vogt and his grenadiers maintained their precarious positions until morning when the spearhead of the advancing German units arrived and secured the bridge.

Vogt was then laid low by an attack of typhus, prevalent in Russia. On his recovery he was posted as an instructor to the SS-Junkerschule Tölz in Bavaria, followed by the Unterführerschule Lauenberg, where prospective officers and NCOs gained the benefits of his now considerable combat experience.

In May 1943, Vogt was promoted to SS-Hauptsturmführer and posted to 3rd SS Panzer Division Totenkopf, serving with SS-Panzer Ausbildungs und Ersatzabteilung 3 for two months before moving to Kraftfahrtechnischen Lehranstalt der Waffen-SS in Vienna. Service in a motor transport training unit was anathema to Vogt and he continually pestered his superiors for a combat posting until they finally relented and in the autumn of 1943 he took command of the Norwegian and Donau-German volunteers in I Bataillon / SS-Freiwillige Panzer Grenadier Regiment 23 Norge, part of III (germanische) Panzer Korps.

By the end of 1943, the Korps lay in the Oranienbaum cauldron.

On 14 January 1944, the Russians began a massive offensive along the front south of Leningrad and on the Wolchow bridgehead. Vogt's battalion, held as Corps reserve, was committed on 17 January along with 1st SS-Grenadier Regiment 24 Danmark, 1st SS-Freiwillige Panzer Grenadier Regiment 48 General Seyffardt and the assault gun detachment from 23rd SS-Freiwillige Panzer Grenadier Division Nederland, thrown into the line to support the area held by the Luftwaffe's Feld-Divisionen – units generally held to be of debatable quality.

In intense, bloody combat the volunteers of Vogt's battalion prevented the breakthrough of the Russians to the Leningrad-Narwa highway. In nightmare battles the Soviets, with overwhelming superiority in manpower, seemingly unending supplies of artillery and mortars as well as ground-attack aircraft, launched countless desperate attacks in their vain efforts to take the road. The highway, however, remained open. Thanks to the sacrifices made by III SS Panzer Korps, the highway was held open long enough for the battered remnant of Eighteenth Army to withdraw to relative safety. During these battles Vogt was constantly to be found in the thick of the fighting, encouraging his men in their almost superhuman efforts. Vogt's men played a major part in holding the highway open.

Battered and decimated by the Soviet winter offensive and the retreat at Narwa, I Bataillon Norge was reformed in April 1944. Vogt, however, was not to return to his regiment, as his battalion was withdrawn from the regiment at the end of the year and posted to Hungary to support 5th SS Panzer Division Wiking.

On 5 January 1945, Vogt's unit was involved in supporting a Wiking mission. An armoured battle group from Wiking was to attempt to force a passage through the Vertes mountains to Budapest and relieve the encircled Germans and Hungarian units of IX SS Gebirgs Korp cut off there. Despite the rigours of the terrain and constant enemy attacks, the group forced its way to Bickse, just 25 kilometres west of their encircled comrades. Too weak to push on to Budapest and with powerful enemy forces approaching fast, the Germans occupied the castle at Gutes Hegyiks and set up their defences. If they could hold this position it would at least block the enemy supply routes.

As darkness fell the Waffen-SS grenadiers awaited the inevitable Russian onslaught. The tanks would be of limited use in night combat, it would be the humble grenadiers who would decide this battle, and only three weakened companies were available. Shortly before midnight the attack began. Heavy infantry concentrations with considerable fire support attacked the Germans on two sides simultaneously and soon the German and Russian opponents were engaged in fierce hand-to-hand combat. It quickly became apparent that the enemy had breached the walls. Men of Vogt's close-combat platoon, held in reserve, counter-attacked and after an hour's ferocious combat with no quarter given or expected on either side, the Soviets were driven off and the walls secured. The enemy however, mounted yet another attack with renewed vigour. Heavy artillery fire and air attacks battered the Germans. For more than 72 hours the Germans had no respite. Then heavy tanks appeared and blasted great gaps in the walls through which the Russian infantry poured. Once again Waffen-SS grenadiers and Russian infantry found themselves in bloody hand-to-hand combat.

As the German forces regrouped and prepared to attempt yet another assault towards Budapest, I SS-Panzer Grenadier Regiment Norge found itself on the left flank of the Panzer Grenadier Regiment of 1st Panzer Division. Army and Waffen-SS comrades fought alongside each other once again in bitter hand-to-hand combat and by the morning of 26 January, the area was secured. By the evening of the same day however, the Russians struck back with heavy armoured support at the German left flank. The brunt of the attack fell on the positions occupied by Vogt's unit. Against such overwhelming odds, Vogt knew that his meagre forces could not hold out, but he was determined to make the enemy pay dearly for every yard of ground. Forming his men into tank-hunting teams, Vogt carried out a fighting withdrawal to the south-west. From a total of some 200 enemy tanks destroyed in this battle, Vogt's unit was responsible for 54 and Vogt personally knocked out three Russian tanks single-handedly. Whether in attack or defence, Vogt led his men with such *élan* and great personal gallantry and disregard for his own safety that his men were inspired to exceptional achievements. On 16 March 1945, Vogt was awarded the Oakleaves to his Knight's Cross for his bravery and leadership. Because of the chaotic conditions at the front, however, the actual award never reached Vogt.

Promoted to SS-Sturmbannführer, Vogt took command of SS-Panzer Aufklärungsabteilung 5, in 5th SS Panzer Division Wiking. At the end of March a Soviet ground-attack fighter strafed the command car in which Vogt was travelling and he was mortally wounded. His commander, SS-Standartenführer Karl Ullrich, took off his own Oakleaves and hung them around the neck of his dying comrade. Vogt had received his Oakleaves at last.

Fritz Vogt was buried in the graveyard near Fürstenfelde, but when the Soviet advance threatened the area his comrades disinterred his body and he was reburied in safety near Graz. His comrades would not allow the possibility of his grave being desecrated by the enemy.

SS-Sturmbannführer Ludwig Kepplinger

Ludwig Kepplinger was born in Linz in December 1911 and began his military career with the Federal Austrian Army in Alpenjäger Regiment 7, but was discharged because of his right wing political beliefs and moved from Austria into Germany, settling in Bavaria. Here, in 1935, he joined the SS-Verfügungstruppe. Within three years he had progressed to the rank of SS-Oberscharführer and section leader in 6 Kompanie of SS-Standarte Deutschland in Munich. Following the Anschluss with Austria, Kepplinger, along with II Bataillon of Standarte Deutschland was transferred to Vienna as a cadre for the newly formed SS-Standarte 'Der Führer'.

By the outbreak of war, Kepplinger had reached the rank of SS-Hauptscharführer, the most senior NCO rank in the Waffen-SS. He first saw combat action with the SS-Verfügungs Division during the Western Campaign as a section leader with 11 Kompanie, 'Der Führer'. He was tasked to take an 18-strong assault group at dawn on 10 May 1940 and attack the Dutch strongpoint at Fort Westervoort on the Issel. From Kepplinger's position to the target was a distance of some eighteen kilometres which the Germans covered, although in almost constant contact with the enemy and under heavy fire, without casualties and even managing to take some twenty prisoners. When they arrived, however, it was to find the bridge over the Issel by the forest had been blown. Kepplinger immediately took the initiative and with two of his men set off to cross the river, scrambling over the twisted wreckage of the bridge. Despite heavy fire, all three made it safely to the other side. Attacking the enemy positions with hand-grenades, Kepplinger and his men showed such ferocity in attack that the enemy were quickly demoralized and began to surrender. More than ninety Dutch soldiers of the garrison surrendered. Shortly afterwards, Kepplinger took on another Dutch bunker on his own and despite enemy fire, quickly neutralized it with hand-grenades. On the same day Kepplinger and two comrades captured thirty more Dutch soldiers. His luck finally run out on the following day when, during an attack on Dutch defensive positions, he received multiple wounds, in the abdomen, thigh and hand. While recovering in hospital he was decorated with both the Second and First Class Iron Crosses.

Unknown to Kepplinger, however, this was but the precursor to an even greater honour. At Westervoort Kepplinger, supported by only two comrades, had crossed the Issel under heavy fire, oblivious of the threats to his own safety, stormed a heavily defended fortress position with such vigour as to achieve its quick surrender and taken ninety prisoners. This achievement had secured the breakthrough of his regiment in rapid time and played no small part in the overall German success in Holland. His grateful superiors had recommended him for the award of the Knight's Cross, which could not be awarded until both of the lower grades had been attained, hence the award of both Second and First Class Iron Crosses at the same time. The recommendation for his Knight's Cross was duly processed and approved, the award being made on 4 September 1940. Kepplinger was the first NCO of the Waffen-SS to receive this high honour.

Shortly afterwards, Kepplinger received a battlefield commission to SS-Untersturmführer and given command of 10 Kompanie, SS Panzer Grenadier Regiment 'Westland', a part of the élite 5th SS Panzer Division 'Wiking'. He then served with distinction on the Eastern Front before a further more serious wound saw him returned to Germany for treatment. Subsequently Kepplinger was posted to II Abteilung of SS Panzer Ersatz Regiment in Riga where he remained until April 1944. At this time, now holding the rank of SS-Sturmbannführer, he was posted to SS Panzer Abteilung 17, in the recently formed 17th SS Panzer Grenadier Division 'Götz von Berlichingen'. This unit spent its entire life on the Western Front. Kepplinger's Abteilung was equipped with the Sturmgeschütz IV, a 75mm assault gun based on the chassis of the Panzer Mk IV. Thrown into the ferocious tank battles of the Normandy bridgehead immediately after the Allied landings, Kepplinger's Abteilung succeeded in knocking out more than forty enemy tanks, though his own losses were severe. Seventeen of his Sturmgeschützen were destroyed by enemy fire and fighter-bomber attacks. By the end of July the division had lost most of its armoured vehicles. The panzer crewmen without tanks assembled at divisional reserve positions behind the lines to regroup.

On 6 August, Kepplinger and his panzer men set off by truck on the return to the front, passing through villages some of which, somewhat prematurely, had already decorated their houses with flowers and bunting to welcome their American liberators. At about 1700 hours, just outside Laval, the truck driver was startled to hear machine-gun fire at close range and immediately pulled his truck on to the verge. Several armed men could be seen running through the fields to their right. The driver turned round to see in horror, that Kepplinger in the seat next to him was slumped forward, his body riddled with bullets one of which had hit him in the temple, killing him instantly. Several other soldiers had been seriously wounded. The surviving Germans attempted to continue their journey, but shortly afterwards were captured when they ran smack into an American tank force. Ludwig Kepplinger was given an honourable burial by the local inhabitants. He was typical of the fearless young commanders of the Waffen-SS who had served in the ranks, and had a superb rapport with his men.

1941

This year saw the great expansion of the territories occupied by the Third Reich. The Wehrmacht moved into the Balkans, occupying Greece and Crete while Rommel's Afrika Korps bolstered the weak Italian forces in North Africa. The greatest of Hitler's military adventures began in June, however, when the German armies were launched into the Soviet Union in Operation 'Barbarossa'. In the ensuing years some of the greatest battles ever fought were enacted in the vastness of the Russian landscape. Tens of millions of men fought a war of unparalleled savagery leaving many millions dead and the country devastated. Although for the most part the war was ferocious, with no quarter given or expected, there were many examples of chivalry and extreme gallantry on both sides.

Here, on the vast Russian plains, the German infantryman came into his own. Now, many Knight's Crosses would be won by junior NCOs and private soldiers who found themselves in situations where only their immediate unselfish actions could save the day, and magnificently rose to the occasion.

The numbers of Knight's Crosses awarded rose dramatically once Operation 'Barbarossa' had commenced. For example during January 1941, a total of ten Knight's Crosses were awarded. For July, August, September and October the figures were 111, 111, 120 and 110 respectively. This was almost as many as had been awarded on all fronts so far. The awards of Oakleaves also soared from an average of about one per month up to July 1941 when thirteen were awarded. This was to be the start of a gradual increase in the number of awards right up to the end of hostilities. This does not necessarily imply that the Knight's Cross became easier to win or that it was in any way liberally issued, but rather it resulted from the ever expanding conflict. With more soldiers fighting more battles on more fronts, the incidence of acts of heroism was bound to increase.

Oberst Harry Herrmann

A Berliner, Harry Herrmann was born on 27 May 1909. Not yet twenty years old, in April 1929, he became a Police Cadet, training at the Polizeischule Brandenburg. On completing his training he joined the Berlin Schutzpolizei. Shortly after the Nazis came to power, Herrmann joined 1 Kompanie, Polzei Abteilung z.b.V. Wecke. This was a special unit under the direct control of Hermann Göring in his capacity as head of the Prussian police. It was composed of men who were felt to be completely reliable and could be depended on in a crisis. Retitled Landespolizeigruppe z.b.V. Wecke in July 1933, by January 1944 it had become Landespolizeigruppe General Göring. This then was the genesis of the huge Fallschirmpanzerkorps Hermann Göring.

From 1 October 1934 until 30 September 1935, Hermann attended the Polizei Offizierschule Eiche, near Potsdam and on completion of this course was commissioned Leutnant and rejoined his unit, now once again retitled – Regiment General Göring. From August 1936 to October 1936, Leutnant Herrmann attended the Fallschirmschule at Stendal to undergo his full paratroops training. This was completed by a second course, from April to May 1937.

On 1 October 1937, Leutnant Herrmann was appointed as adjutant to I Bataillon, Regiment General Göring, a position he held for six months before transferring as adjutant to I Bataillon, Fallschirmjäger Regiment 1. On 1 January 1938, Herrmann had been promoted to Oberleutnant. One year later, in January 1939, he became the regimental adjutant for a short period before joining the staff of the parachute training school at Stendal.

On 1 August 1939, Herrmann was appointed orderly officer on the staff of 7th Flieger Division. The division was still not fully formed on the outbreak of war and did not take part in the Polish Campaign. Herrmann, however, saw action during the invasion of Holland, where the division's two Fallschirmjäger regiments took part in a number of successful raids on bridges, airfields and other essential targets. For his part in the campaign in Holland Herrmann was awarded the Iron Cross Second Class and First Class on 22 May 1940. On 1 June, Oberleutnant Herrmann took command of 5 Kompanie, Fallschirmjäger Regiment 1 in Tangermünde.

Herrmann next saw combat during the aerial assault on Crete. On 20 May 1941, Herrmann jumped with the men of his Kompanie near Karteros in the vicinity of the airfield at Heraklion. This airfield was one of the principal targets of the regiment, its capture being essential to the subsequent reinforcement of the first assault wave. Paratroops dropping slowly into the centre of a battlefield are at a terrible risk from ground fire, a fate suffered later in the war by the Polish paratroopers at Arnhem. As he gently floated towards earth, Oberleutnant Herrmann suffered a severe head wound and was temporarily blinded. At times losing consciousness, he nevertheless rallied his men, guided by the company sergeant-major, Hauptfeldwebel Kurth, and his orderly. In the course of the assault, both men fell, fighting by his side. As twilight approached Oberleutnant Herrmann crawled, able only to differentiate between shades of dark and light, in the direction of the setting sun, taking him towards his objective, the airfield. Only after relief troops arrived during the following morning could Oberleutnant Herrmann be taken to the regimental command post for medical treatment. Luckily, Herrmann recovered completely from his wound.

This gallant Fallschirmjäger, despite being disabled not just by the pain of his wound but by the almost total loss of sight, and drifting in and out of consciousness, had shown great heroism in continuing to lead his men into the assault against heavily defended enemy positions. He was recommended for the Knight's Cross of the Iron Cross with the comment 'he has given his brave paratroopers a shining example of gallantry and loyalty in a very grave situation'. Oberleutnant Harry Herrmann joined the ranks of the *Ritterkreuzträger* on 9 July 1941.

On recovering from his wounds he was posted to command 1 Kompanie, of the paratroop training battalion at Döberitz. He was also promoted to Hauptmann on the direct orders of Reichsmarschall Göring, further reward for his gallant actions. He remained with the training battalion until 1 May 1942 when he was posted to the Staff of XI Flieger Korps. This corps was responsible for planning airborne operations and the development of special equipment and weapons for the airborne arm. On 1 April 1942, Herrmann was promoted to Major.

German participation in the campaign in North Africa had shown the High Command that a high-quality mobile reserve was required and this task fell to XI Flieger Korps which was moved into the area around Avignon. All sorts of new weapons, equipment, new camouflaged clothing, etc., was introduced, and the Fallschirmjäger trained up to a new peak of efficiency. Morale was at an all-time high. The Korps controlled 1 and 2 Fallschirm Divisions and was responsible for planning the takeover of Rome following the Italian capitulation, and for the operation to free Mussolini.

On 21 September 1943, Herrmann was appointed to command Fallschirmjäger Lehr Bataillon. Continuing to serve on the Italian Front, the battalion saw fierce fighting against the Allies at the Nettuno bridgehead. Herrmann's paratroops showed such daring and gallantry that they were mentioned in official Wehrmacht dispatches. 'In the heavy fighting during the past weeks in the bridgehead at Nettuno, Fallschirmjäger Lehr Bataillon under the leadership of Major Herrmann has particularly distinguished itself.'

In June 1944, Major Herrmann was appointed to command Fallschirm Jager Lehr Regiment 21 seeing action during the Normandy battles. On 22 July 1944 he was awarded the German Cross in Gold.

Following heavy losses in the Normandy battles, 6 Fallschirm Division was broken down into smaller Kampfgruppen, one of which was to be commanded by Herrmann, promoted to Oberstleutnant in August 1944. Kampfgruppe Herrmann fought in Holland during the retreat and withdrawal into the Reichswald. In February 1945, he took command of a paratroop tank-hunting unit, Fallschirm Panzer Jagd Brigade (Herrmann) before, on 19 April, being given command of 9 Fallschirm Division with the rank of Oberst.

In the last few weeks of the war, Oberst Herrmann found himself defending his home town of Berlin against the Russian onslaught. On 2 May he was taken into captivity and languished as a prisoner of the Russians for more than ten years. His strength of character, so ably displayed during five years of hard combat, helped him to keep his morale intact through these difficult years of imprisonment.

Post-war, Herrmann rejoined the armed forces when the West German Bundeswehr was formed. He was deputy commander of 1 Luftlande Division and became commander of the Luftlande-Lufttransportschule in Altenstadt before finally retiring in 1967.

Oberstarzt Dr Heinrich Neumann

Born in the Steglitz area of Berlin on 17 February 1908, Dr Neumann began his military career at the age of 24 when, in January 1933, he enlisted in the army, joining 15 Kompanie, Infanterie Regiment 9, and began his training for the medical corps. By 1 May he had been promoted to Unterarzt and one month later joined 6 (Preussische) Sanitäts Abteilung of the Sanitäts Staffel Braunschweig before moving on to 1 Kompanie, Infanterie Regiment 17.

While still engaged in his medical training, undertaking degree studies at the University of Münster, he was transferred from the army to the Luftwaffe in March 1934. On 1 April he was assigned to the Flieger Sanitäts Staffel Braunschweig as Assistenzarzt. On 18 June 1934, Neumann graduated from Münster University as a Doctor of Medicine. He was also commissioned with the military rank of Oberarzt.

In November 1934, Dr Neumann underwent training as member of aircrew personnel when he attended Observers' training at the Aufklärer Fliegerschule Braunschweig before being posted to Berlin as Fliegerstandortarzt – a Luftwaffe Garrison Doctor – in February of 1935. In July he attended the Fliegerschule at Staaken for training as a pilot and in August was promoted to Stabsarzt.

In December 1936, Neumann joined the German contingent supporting Franco's forces during the Spanish Civil War, the notorious Legion Condor. He served as an Observer with Jagdgruppe 88, flying the Heinkel He 51. Returning from Spain in 1938, he served in his medical capacity variously with Luftgau Sanitäts Abteilung 1, Luftwaffen Sanitäts Staffel Königsberg and as Standortarzt with 1 Abteilung of Flak Regiment 1. In late August 1938, Dr Neumann joined the staff of Flieger Division 7 as Adjutant to the Divisional Physician. As a member of the staff of a Paratroop unit, Neumann underwent full paratrooper training at the Fallschirmjäger training grounds at Stendal, and earned his paratrooper's wings.

During 1939, Dr Neumann served with a number of Luftwaffe medical units. In June he was decorated with the Spanish Cross in Silver with Swords to recognize his service during the Spanish Civil War with the Legion Condor. The Spanish also decorated him with the Medalla de la Campana and the Cruz de Guerra. He was also promoted to Oberstabsarzt – equivalent to the military rank of Major, in May 1939. In July 1939, he was posted as the head of the Luftwaffe Medical Company in Flieger Division 7.

During the invasion of the Low Countries, Neumann served with the Division in Holland where his men succeeded in disarming the guards at the Süder military hospital and capturing it without bloodshed, and also in flushing out the Dutch sniper training school opposite. For this he was awarded both Second and First Class Iron Crosses on 20 May 1940. By the end of 1940, Dr Neumann was serving on the Staff of the Regimental Physician of Fallschirm Sturm Regiment 1.

In 1941, Hitler had been persuaded that the capture of Crete and its airfields was essential to German operations in the Balkans. It was decided that an airborne assault be launched with Fallschirmjäger and glider-borne troops supported by Gebirgsjäger under the command of mountain troop Generalleutnant Julius Ringel, to be flown in in Junkers Ju 52 transports. German Intelligence had grossly underestimated the size of the Allied garrison and were unaware that the astute New Zealander General Freyberg, had accurately assessed the likely landing places for any likely German attack and had had these sites heavily defended.

During the attack, Fallschirmjäger Sturm Regiment 1 was tasked to capture Maleme airfield and on 20 May 1941 after a preliminary attack by Junkers Ju 87 Stuka dive-bombers, the glider force was flown in. The defenders, however, were well dug in, in well-chosen and camouflaged positions, most of which survived the dive-bombing attack unscathed. The glider-borne troops were met by a murderous hail of fire and suffered heavy casualties. Almost immediately the commander of I Bataillon, Major Walter Koch, tasked with the capture of the anti-aircraft positions overlooking the airfield on Hill 107, was disabled by a serious head wound. In fact every officer in the Bataillon was wounded to some extent. It was left to the medical officer, Dr Neumann, to take command of the remnant. He could see the carnage being caused by the enemy guns and determined to push ahead with what troops he had left and attempt to storm the hill. Personally leading his tough paras, Dr Neumann pushed forward his attack with great determination, but heavy defensive fire prevented him from reaching the top of the hill.

So powerful and aggressive had been his attempts, however, that the Allies feared their forward companies had been overrun and under cover of darkness on the night of 20/21 May, started to withdraw. With only a rearguard force left behind on the hill, Dr Neumann was able to force his way up to the top of the hill on 21 May and capture the enemy positions with its guns intact. These guns were now turned on their former owners and took out several targets on the airfield, the respite allowing the Luftwaffe to land supplies and munitions by Ju 52.

For his own personal gallantry in leading the attack on the Allied positions and the success he achieved, Neumann was recommended for the Knight's Cross of the Iron Cross by Oberst Bernhard Hermann Ramcke, the commander of the regiment, after its original commander, Generalmajor Meindl, had been wounded. In Ramcke's view – 'The determination of Oberstabsarzt Dr Neumann, with only limited forces to attack the north-west face of Hill 107 which threatened Maleme airfield with its well-sited anti-aircraft guns, proved decisive to the battle. Misled by the violence of the assault the enemy withdrew from the hill during the night. At dawn the rearguard was thrown from the hill in an assault led by Neumann. As an outstanding individual combatant, he fulfilled his role as Regimental Physician in gallant actions ... ' Neumann's Knight's Cross was awarded on 21 August 1941.

After Crete, the much weakened Flieger Division 7 was to require considerable reinforcement and rebuilding before it could be sent into action again. Indeed Hitler was so upset by the German losses that he refused to countenance any further large-scale parachute operations for the rest of the war.

In late 1942, Dr Neumann was posted to Division Meindl as Divisional Physician. This division was an *ad hoc* unit formed from a variety of Luftwaffe field units under the overall command of Generalmajor Eugen Meindl. It fought with great determination in the area of the eastern front between Staraya Russa and Juchnow. More than 3,000 battle hardened veteran paras perished during the winter battles of 1942/43, first-class soldiers who could not easily be replaced.

In June 1944, Dr Neumann, by now an Oberstarzt – full colonel – was appointed Divisional Physician to the newly formed Fallschirm-jäger Division 6. Formed in the Amiens area of France, its main elements were 16, 17 and 18 Fallschirmjäger Regiments under command of Generalmajor Plocher. Dr Neumann saw combat service during the Normandy battles with the new division which fought well but suffered heavy losses, especially during the Allied breakout from the Normandy bridgehead area in July. Neumann and his medical staff were certainly kept busy during these hectic days. On 1 August Oberstarzt Dr Neumann was appointed Korpsarzt of II Fallschirm Korps, the parent corps of 6, 7 and 8 Fallschirmjäger Divisions and served in Holland, and opposing the Allied crossing of the Rhine. Withdrawing into north-west Germany, the Corps eventually surrendered to the British in April 1945.

After the war, in 1959, Dr Neumann joined the new West German Bundeswehr as a medical officer, retaining his old rank of Oberstarzt. Re-qualifying for his jump wings, he served until 1964 before finally retiring. He is still alive.

1942

B y 1942, the mid point of the war, German expansion had reached its zenith. Despite being badly battered by the Russian winter offensive, with only eight out of 162 divisions still at full strength by March, and losses totalling more than a million men, the Germans rallied and by May had regained the initiative. Russian losses stood at more than seven million, but these could be more easily made good, whereas the German Army was beginning to be bled dry. As the summer wore on the German armies approached Stalingrad and things looked bad for the Russians.

In North Africa Rommel's desert army had scored some outstanding successes against the British. This unique campaign was fought, unlike that on the Eastern Front, with a considerable degree of chivalry on both sides, the opposing armies having a great deal of respect and even a deal of admiration for the fighting qualities of each other.

As winter approached, however, Hitler's forces on the Eastern Front and in North Africa began to run out of steam, their supply lines over-extended and faced by the considerable *matériel* superiority of the enemy.

A massive Russian counter-offensive at Stalingrad saw the annihilation of Sixth Army under Generalfeldmarschall Paulus. The tide had turned and from now on any victories would be only temporary and the Wehrmacht could now only delay and not prevent, eventual defeat. The German soldier would be called upon to make ever greater efforts and ever greater sacrifices. Now acts of gallantry earning the Knight's Cross were, with ever greater frequency, for defensive actions. Some 952 Knight's Crosses were awarded during 1942, averaging about 80 per month. The greatest number were awarded in the latter part of the year for defensive actions after the Soviets launched their winter offensive, with 135 awards in September, 113 in October and 124 in December. Oakleaves awards were also high during these months at 15, 12 and 19 respectively. The next highest grade, the Swords, continued to be awarded very sparingly, still only averaging two per month.

SS-Oberführer Karl Ullrich

Born on 1 December 1910 in Saargemünd, Karl Ullrich was the son of a Finance Official. He attended Realschule in Bad Kissingen followed by two years practical training with an engineering company – Maschinenfabrik Augsburg–Nürnberg, and an electrical company – Elektrizitätswek Bad Kissingen before attending the Höheren Technischen Staatslehranstalten for three years to study engineering. In 1933 he qualified as a mechanical engineer.

Ullrich's distinguished military career began when he joined the SS in 1932. In 1933 he volunteered for military service and became a soldier with Infanterie Regiment 19 in the Reichswehr for three months' basic military training at Grafenwöhr before joining the SS-Verfügungstruppe (service in the SS-Verfügungstruppe could count as the equivalent of national service with the Reichswehr).

In July 1934, he became an NCO with 1 Kompanie / SS-Standarte 1 in München. In March 1935 he was selected for officer training at the SS-Junkerschule Braunschweig and was eventually commissioned SS-Untersturmführer in April 1936. Then followed a course of training at the Army's Pioniereschule in Dessau to exploit his engineering background, after which, on 1 September 1937, he was promoted to SS-Obersturmführer and was given command of 3 Kompanie of the SS-Pioniersturmbann. Ullrich saw service with the SS-Verfügungstruppe during the occupation of Austria and the Sudetenland and by the outbreak of war had been promoted to SS-Hauptsturmführer.

During the Polish campaign, he saw combat action with his SS-Pioniersturmbann, being attached to an army division. In 1940, the Western Campaign found him and his Pioniere serving with distinction with the SS-Verfügungsdivision, successfully clearing minefields and bridging canals and rivers. So fast was the German advance that the Pioniere were forced to work under intense pressure, not to mention danger. In recognition of his achievements during this campaign, Ullrich was decorated with both the Second and First Class Iron Crosses.

Remaining with his Pioniere during the invasion of Greece, he was subsequently posted to the SS-Totenkopf Division in May 1941, where he took command of SS-Pioniere Bataillon 3.

Allocated to the northern sector of the Eastern Front after the German invasion of the Soviet Union in June 1941, Ullrich's unit once again distinguished itself during the attack on the heavily defended bunkers of the Stalin Line near Sebesh, and through the forests of Brianskaja.

In January 1942 the Russians launched a powerful counter-offensive with two Guard Corps storming down from the north over the frozen swamps. From the south, three Shock Armies punched into the Germans. The German II Armeekorps staggered back. In this critical situation, Ullrich, commanding a small Kampfgruppe in Staraya Russa, under control of the army's 18th Infanterie Division, was thrown into battle at Kobylkina. It was essential that Ullrich's Kampfgruppe hold their defensive positions and the bridge over the River Lowat at Korowitschina to give them a base from which to launch attacks on the enemy's vital supply routes. After a week's fighting the Germans were cut off and had to be resupplied by air. The Russians launched countless assaults on the Germans. Lined up against their meagre forces were three Soviet Guards Regiments, two battalions of Ski Troops and some thirty tanks.

Russian bombardments had destroyed virtually all cover and the SS-Pioniere huddled in their dugouts in 45 degrees of frost. Cold and hungry, the men of Kampfgruppe Ullrich nevertheless defended their territory with great courage and fortitude. Bombarded by artillery fire, mortars, dive-bombing attacks, tank fire and massed infantry attacks – often as many as five massed assaults in one day's combat – the Germans resisted all attempts to dislodge them. The Russians were often driven off only after bitter hand-to-hand fighting. It is beyond doubt that one of the major factors in the determined resistance put up by the Germans was the personal example of Karl Ullrich. Always calm and composed despite the desperate situation, his steadfastness and confidence, his concern for his men's welfare and his own gallantry gave them strength to hold out. Ullrich was not the type of commander to be found safe in a dugout to the rear but would always be found in the thick of the fighting alongside his men.

On 19 February a radio message informed Ullrich that he had been awarded the Knight's Cross of the Iron Cross. His reply was that he would much rather have more fresh troops than a decoration. Finally given the authority to attempt a breakout, Kampfgruppe Ullrich fought its way out of the encirclement on the night of 22/23 February, leaving nearly 2,000 enemy dead lying on the battlefield in the area around Kobylkino.

Having shown great qualities of gallantry leadership and organization at Kobylkino, Ullrich was appointed commander of Pionere for the entire SS-Panzerkorps and served in this position during the winter battles of 1942/43 around Kharkov. In March 1943 at his own request he was transferred back to the Totenkopf Division and took command of III / SS Panzer Grenadier Regiment 5.

On 10 July 1943, the Totenkopf Division took part in an attack over the Pssel, tasked to form a bridgehead on the enemy side. The assault quickly foundered, however, under concentrated enemy artillery and mortar fire. Totenkopf's own artillery was unable to give effective cover as it had no artillery observers on the enemy side of the river to spot targets. Despite this, Ullrich and his men pressed forward, capturing the enemy-held village of Krassnyj Oktjobr and forming a small bridgehead. The Russians launched countless infantry and tank assaults in a vain attempt to drive out the Germans. Ullrich and his men held the bridgehead for a full seven days, allowing the division to secure a launch-point for its part in the massive Kursk offensive. The Totenkopf Division was badly battered during this ill-fated Operation 'Zitadelle', losing half its tanks and vehicles and suffering heavy casualties.

In November 1943, Ullrich was promoted to Obersturmbann-führer and appointed to command SS Panzer Grenadier Regiment 6 Theodor Eicke just as the regiment was coming under furious Russian attacks. III Bataillon was being pushed back to the east edge of Bairak and the situation was desperate, but Ullrich calmly and quickly assembled an assault force from his last remaining reserves and launched an immediate counter-attack. Within a few hours the enemy had been repulsed and a breakthrough foiled. The regiment had just cause to thank its new commander. Once again his calm confident manner in a crisis had spurred his men on to great efforts and saved the day. His reputation as a gallant comrade with a genuine concern for the welfare of his men grew daily. Throughout the battles of 1943/44 he continued to inspire his men to achieve what seemed to be unachievable. In early March 1944 the Russians succeeded in breaking through in a neighbouring sector. On his own initiative, Ullrich quickly gathered an *ad hoc* force from whatever troops could be spared. On the following day he personally led his men into a successful counter-attack which halted the enemy breakthrough. On 14 May 1944, Ullrich was decorated with the Oakleaves to his Knight's Cross.

On 29 July 1944 Ullrich was promoted to SS-Standartenführer. On 9 October, he took command of the élite 5th SS Panzer Division Wiking which, with the Totenkopf Division made up IV SS Panzer Korps. The corps served on the northern sector of the Eastern Front, attempting to hold back the Russians before Warsaw, destroying hundreds of enemy tanks in massive battles before being rushed south to Hungary in December.

Here the corps was to strike east towards Budapest and relieve the trapped German forces surrounded there, including two SS units – 8 SS Kavallerie Division Florian Geyer and 22 SS Freiwilligen Kavallerie Division Maria Theresia. On 1 January 1945, Wiking struck east over the most difficult terrain and against strong enemy defences, reaching Bielcze on 5 January. A Kampfgruppe was detached to make contact with the encircled units in Budapest. After a promising start the push was halted by Hitler and the SS troops moved south to renew the attack from that direction. It was too late, however; the attack failed and Budapest was lost.

By February Wiking was in the area around Stuhlweissenburg and took part in the last great offensive of the war when Sixth SS Panzer Army attempted a counter-offensive around Lake Balaton. This attack was quickly blunted by the enemy, however, and soon the Germans were reeling back under the renewed Russian advance. Wiking lost contact with its left-hand neighbouring unit and found its supply routes cut. As III Panzer Korps began to withdraw, Ullrich made the unauthorized decision to withdraw his troops too, and broke out towards the west.

The 9th SS Panzer Division Hohenstaufen, under SS-Brigade-führer Sylvester Stadler, was at that time fighting gallantly to hold open the jaws of the Russian pincer movement to the north of the Plattensee. Stuhlweissenburg had by now lost its strategic significance, a fact plain to all the troops on the ground if not to the high command. By ignoring a specific Führer-Order to stand fast, Ullrich could quickly find himself facing a death sentence, but he saw no reason to sacrifice his men in a pointless defence of an area no longer of importance. Wiking now conducted a fighting withdrawal into Austria and took part in the defence of Vienna. Ullrich was promoted to SS-Oberführer on 20 April 1945. Just three weeks later he was a prisoner of war, captured by the Americans.

Karl Ullrich was one of the finest soldiers of the Waffen-SS. Great personal gallantry together with leadership qualities of the highest order brought Ullrich the devotion of his men. The morale of units under his command remained high until the bitter end.

Karl Ullrich survived the war and imprisonment and now lives in retirement.

Leutnant Hans Sturm

Hans Sturm was born in Dortmund on 29 July 1920, the son of an engineer. After leaving school he studied metal working and attended both day and evening courses at the State Engineering Schools in Dortmund and Aachen. His civilian career, however, was cut short on 3 October 1940 when, not long after his twentieth birthday, he was called up for military service.

Sturm had earlier been a member of the Marine Hitler Jugend where he developed a particular interest in signals. He had attained both the A- and B-Prüfung but to qualify for the C-Prüfung, the highest grade, he was required to take part in a world training cruise in one of the Kriegsmarine's school ships. His father refused permission, arguing that it would interfere too much with his training as an engineer.

Now that he was to be enrolled for military service, his recruiting officer seemed determined that Sturm should join his Heavy Flak detachment in Dortmund. In the end, thanks to a typical bureaucratic decision that ignored his naval training, he was posted to the infantry where he joined Infanterie Ersatz Bataillon 289 in Herford to undergo his three weeks' induction into the Wehrmacht.

On 29 October Sturm was given his first posting to a combat unit, joining Infanterie Regiment 473, a part of 253rd Infanterie Division. After two months in the Recruit Company, he joined the unit on occupation duty in France, where it remained until the spring of 1941 when it was transferred to Poland in preparation for the invasion of the Soviet Union.

The unit entered Russia in June 1941 and took part in the assault on Moscow. Within a few weeks Sturm had seen a considerable amount of action and for distinguishing himself during combat actions, on 29 July, his 21st birthday, he was decorated with the Iron Cross Second Class. Sturm, however, was unaware of the award which had been made by his unit for his steadfast gallantry under fire when serving in a small assault group. After a further display of selfless determination during a powerful enemy attack near Welikie Luki on the night of 31 July/1 August he was summoned before his Company Commander and presented with his Iron Cross. His smiling Commander told him 'You have already earned the Iron Cross Second Class. Now I will recommend you for the First Class.' The Battalion Commander then stepped forward and pinned his own Iron Cross First Class on to the astonished Sturm's tunic, 'on loan' until Sturm's Cross was approved. This duly occurred and Sturm's Iron Cross First Class was officially awarded, effective 1 August. Sturm was rapidly gaining a reputation as a first-class, dependable soldier.

On 22 August he was wounded in action for the first time, by hand-grenade splinters during close-quarter fighting, and was decorated with the Wound Badge in Black. Shortly after this, on 1 September, he was rewarded with a battlefield promotion to Gefreiter. That December he qualified for his Infantry Assault Badge, and in early 1942 he received the Campaign Medal for the Winter Battles in the East.

During this period the division had fought in numerous defensive battles as the Soviets launched a winter offensive; during January Sturm's division had been encircled to the south of Lake Volga and only managed to break out with heavy casualties. On 26 August 1942, Sturm was decorated with the German Cross in Gold, in recognition of further acts of gallantry during fierce fighting when his small assault group attempted an almost suicidal attack on a heavily defended enemy position. During the action, Sturm had risked his own life to save a badly wounded comrade. Only a handful of German soldiers survived the attack. Although Sturm's award was dated 26 August, he did not in fact receive his German Cross until November of that year, after the award of the Knight's Cross.

On the night of 13/14 September 1942, Sturm's unit lay near the banks of the Volga by Rschew. The Russians had determined to break through the German lines and it was against the division's positions that the weight of the main enemy assault would fall. For two days and nights the Germans suffered a furious softening-up barrage and the troops were forced to huddle low in their prepared positions as countless heavy artillery shells and Katyusha rockets howled overhead.

Sturm's regiment was located in an old brickworks on the northern edge of Rschew. As the barrage bore down on them, the medics scuttled to and fro tending the many wounded; meanwhile, concentrated machine-gun fire could be heard coming from the positions held by 3 Platoon who were obviously under enemy attack. As company runner, Sturm was ordered to check out what was happening at 3 Platoon's positions and report back. He quickly dodged his way through to 3 Platoon and found them beseiged by a Russian assault group, hurling grenades as they advanced ever closer. Sturm jumped into the nearest foxhole only to find its occupants dead; then he heard the distinctive rapid fire of a German MG-34 machine-gun and made his way to its position. As he approached the machine-gun nest, a grenade scored a direct hit on it. Sturm entered, to find his two comrades, Löffler and Sandkühler, dead. As bullets began to zip through the air around his position, Sturm threw himself down at the MG-34 and opened fire. The 'Urrah!' cries of the Russians could be clearly heard as they approached ever nearer. Suddenly, Sturm's gun fell silent, his ammunition belt expended. He quickly grabbed some hand-grenades and lobbed them at the approaching enemy, using the few seconds' grace this achieved to feed a new ammunition belt into his machine-gun.

Belt after belt rattled through the machine-gun as Sturm struggled to keep the Russians at bay, some reaching within thirty feet of his position before being cut down. Each time Sturm successfully halted one wave of assault troops a fresh wave took its place. Then he heard the chilling sound of an approaching T-34 tank; its steel bulk would not be held back by a mere machine-gun and as its shells began to fall around his position, he realized that he could not remain where he was for much longer. Taking the MG-34, Sturm ran off to the right and jumped into another foxhole, quickly opening fire again. Several times he changed his position, confusing the enemy as to exactly how many machine-gun positions were firing at them.

Then a Russian 76mm tank shell crashed nearby and Sturm was

blasted from his machine-gun with shell splinters lodged in his hands, shoulder and face. Well aware of the dire situation he was in, he blindly – and agonizingly – groped his way to the miraculously undamaged MG-34 and fed a fresh belt of ammunition into it. Unable to see the enemy due to his wounds, he aimed at the sounds of their cries and resumed fire, determined to go down fighting. Then, just as he was about to be overrun, relief platoons from the company arrived and the enemy were driven off after further fierce fighting.

In the morning, when the full significance of Sturm's actions became apparent, his Regimental Commander, Oberstleutnant Schmidt, informed the Commanding General of 6 Infanterie Division, under whose command the regiment had fought, that Sturm had single-handedly prevented the encirclement of the Regiment and thereby halted the Russian breakthrough.

'This Sturm! He has single-handedly prevented the encirclement of the Regiment and halted the Russian breakthrough. This, Herr General, is worthy of the highest decoration.'

'He will get it Schmidt, I guarantee it,' replied the General.

Meanwhile, the seriously wounded Sturm had been taken to Field Hospital 2/615 in Smolensk where his wounds received treatment from a skilled eye surgeon. Delicate surgery was required to remove the steel slivers which had penetrated his eye; the fragments were taken out but only time would tell if his eyesight had been saved. For ten agonizing days, Sturm lay in total darkness, his eyes heavily bandaged. On the tenth day the dressings were removed and then, as he began to focus, came one of the greatest sights he would ever see – the rays of the sun shining through the ward window. His eyesight had been saved. On 29 September, as Sturm lay asleep in his hospital bed, one of his ward-mates heard the following radio report: 'The Commander-in-Chief has awarded the Knight's Cross of the Iron Cross to Gefreiter Sturm, company runner in an infantry regiment on the Eastern Front. Sturm has excelled himself in the bitter defensive battle near Rschew in that he stood alone despite severe wounds and halted an enemy breakthrough, inflicting bloody losses.'

Sturm's comrade hurried to waken him with the news, but the dazed young Gefreiter refused to believe it. 'You're still dreaming,' he insisted to his friend. Soon the ward sister and other medical personnel arrived to greet the young hero but still he could not believe it. Only when the head surgeon arrived to add his personal congratulations did Sturm finally accept that he had indeed joined the ranks of the *Ritterkreuzträger*.

On 4 October in a small ceremony at the hospital, the presentation was made and the Knight's Cross of the Iron Cross was hung around Sturm's neck. He also received the Wound Badge in Silver and a field promotion to Unteroffizier. After his release from hospital, Sturm was given well-deserved home leave, his first in sixteen months of constant combat action on the Eastern Front. On his return he joined the regimental reserve in Aachen and for a period of just over one year he travelled around the VI and X Military Districts, near Münster and Kassel, giving talks on front-line life to various meetings of factory workers. He also served as a career adviser for NCO and officer candidates; but he was desperate to rejoin his comrades at the front, although all his applications to do so were rejected.

In late 1943 Sturm fell into conversation with an army Oberst during a train journey and mentioned his wish to get back to the front. Much impressed by this brave young soldier, the Oberst agreed that he would certainly like to have him in his unit which was serving in Italy. The Oberst used his influence and, on 15 January, Unteroffizier Sturm found himself standing before Generalmajor Rohr to be told that he was going to Italy. He joined Infanterie Regiment 871, part of 356 Infanterie Division at Ponte Decimo, north of Genoa. Sturm served on the regimental staff where his engineering background came in most useful and he was nominated NCO in charge of the construction of defensive positions.

It was during his spell of duty in Italy that Sturm had one of his most unpleasant experiences. The Pioniere platoon had been assigned as escort troops for a large supply column which was to pass through difficult terrain in which partisans were known to be operating. While moving through a steep-sided pass, the column came under attack and was decimated, with the escort troops also suffering heavy casualties. Sturm led a rescue group in armoured scout cars which, thanks to his considerable experience on the Eastern Front, managed to drive off the partisans. It was then that things turned nasty. The Germans, furious at their losses and in no mood for conciliation, having discovered that some German deserters had joined the partisans, rounded up a number of suspect civilians and, after interrogation, shot several of them. Although he himself took no part in this, Sturm was deeply affected by it. He had taken part in some of the most furious hand-to-hand combat on the Eastern Front where death was always but a moment away and quarter rarely given or expected. He could not, however, accept the cold-blooded execution of civilians who may well have been innocent. He was so upset by this event that he refused to wear the Anti-Partisan Badge he was awarded after the battle; this led to a serious reprimand from his regimental commander and he was fortunate that his moral stand on this issue did not have more serious consequences.

This was by no means his last conflict with the authorities. From June to August 1944 Sturm attended the Hagenau War School in preparation for taking his commission. These were critical times with the Allied invasion of Normandy in June followed by the attempt on Hitler's life in July 1944, fostering a growing paranoia in some circles, with the Gestapo hunting for anyone even remotely connected with defeatist elements. No one could afford to have a loose tongue as even the most innocent remark might be misinterpreted.

No fool, Sturm could clearly see which way the war was going and during a discussion on tactics stated his view that the war should be ended. One of his 'comrades' reported this 'defeatism' and Sturm was dragged before a so-called Council of Honour. His life was now at stake as his offence was punishable by death. However some senior officers who knew of Sturm's gallantry in the field had more sense and General Regener quickly moved to have the proceedings quashed. On 1 September 1944, Sturm was commissioned Leutnant and joined Grenadier Ersatz Bataillon 88 in Fulda. Shortly afterwards, in November, he was transferred to Grafenwöhr as an instructor for Battalion Commanders of the Volkssturm, Hitler's Home Guard, a post he held until January 1945. The following month, Sturm was appointed Special Representative to the Leadership Staff of the Volkssturm. His unpopular task was to travel the Reich forming units from all available manpower. Many of the Nazi Party's officials, nick-named 'Golden Pheasants' because of their gold braid bedecked uniforms, were horrified to find themselves press-ganged into combat units by men such as Sturm just when they were about to go underground to save themselves in the face of the enemy onslaught.

The closing days of the war found Leutnant Sturm in command of one of the many *ad hoc* Kampfgruppen which arose during the defence of Berlin. His 'men' were no longer the tough infantrymen with whom he had served on the Eastern Front and in Italy; now, at least three-quarters of his strength was comprised of young boys from the Hitler Jugend. With such young lads Sturm was even more conscious of the importance of setting a good example; if these impressionable and inexperienced boys were not to panic they would need to be led with both firmness and consideration for their youth. Sturm led them in numerous attacks against the Russians, stalking enemy tanks through the Cottbus forest with Panzerfaust anti-tank weapons. Watching them, wide-eyed in fear and anticipation, with their oversized great-coats and helmets, he determined that no lives were to be squandered in pointless heroics at this late stage of the war and his main task would be to see that as many as possible survived.

As the Russians pushed into Berlin, Sturm's force was stranded by the now famous East-West crossing-point, the Glienicke Bridge, and the Wansee station. On the night of 2 May 1945, Sturm was ordered to make a dash over the bridge towards the station with his remaining troops, but he and his men ran straight into a Russian motorized

ight: A gallant and ~~aring~~ Cavalryman, Georg ~~1~~ichael's quick thinking ~~:~~sulted in the surrender ~~f~~ a much larger enemy ~~r~~ce during the campaign ~~in~~ France. (See page 29).

ight: Paratroop hero ~~1~~ajor Rudolf Witzig, ~~a~~warded the Knight's ~~r~~oss for the attack on the ~~B~~elgian fortress of Eben ~~m~~ael. (See page 33).

Left: Major Michael Pössinger. Note the traditional Edelweiss arm patch of the Mountain Troops on the right sleeve (See page 36.)

Left: SS-Sturmbannführer Fritz Vogt, bearer of both the Knight's Cross and the Oakleaves in recognition of personal gallantry. (See page 40.)

Above:
SS-Sturmbannführer
Ludwig Kepplinger, seen
here in his black Panzer
uniform from his time
with SS-Panzer Abteilung
17. (See page 45.)

Above right: Oberst
Harry Herrmann, here
seen as a Hauptmann
shortly after the award of
his Knight's Cross. (See
page 47.)

Right: Oberstarzt Dr.
Heinrich Neumann, one
of the few medical officers
of the Wehrmacht to be
highly decorated during
the Second World War.
(See page 50.)

Above left: Hans Sturm, a Gefreiter at the time of his award, seen here after being commissioned Leutnant in September 1944. (See page 59.)

Above: Leutnant Bruno Sassen. Note the Fallschirmjäger badge on the breast pocket and the Kreta commemorative cuff-title. (See page 66.)

Left: SS-Oberführer Karl Ullrich. Note the Demjansk arm shield and the Regimental cuff-band Theodor Eicke, on the left sleeve. (See page 56.)

Right: Oberst Martin Steglich, here a Hauptmann in January 1943. Note the German Cross in gold on the right breast pocket. (See page 72.)

Above left: Hauptmann Gerd Mischke, one of but a handful of Fallschirmjäger awarded the Knight's Cross in North Africa. (See page 75.)

Above: Leutnant Wilhelm Wegener, seen here as an Oberwachtmeister. He wears the General Assault Badge on his left breast pocket. (See page 78.)

Left: SS-Unterscharführer Remi Schrynen was one of a very small number of non-Germans to be decorated with the Knight's Cross. (See page 82.)

Right: A highly popular officer, SS-Hauptsturmführer Georg Karck was killed in an automobile accident on his way to the front line. (See page 84.)

Below: SS-Untersturmführer Alfred Schneidereit, seen here shortly after the award of his Knight's Cross and promotion to SS-Unterscharführer. (See page 89.)

Below right: Major Günther Hochgartz as well as being a Knight's Cross winner, held three tank destruction badges for single handedly destroying enemy tanks. (See page 94.)

Left: A soldier with a long and distinguished military career, Major Ferdinand Foltin is seen here in service dress uniform. (See page 97.)

Below left: SS-Major Siegfried Jamrowski, indomitable paratroop officer, decorated with the Knight's Cross for actions at Monte Cassino. (See page 101.)

Below: SS-Unterscharführer Emil Dürr, a brave NCO who sacrificed his life to save his comrades during the Normandy battle. (See page 104.)

Right: Oberleutnant Erich Lepkowski, veteran of the Russian Front, was awarded the Knight's Cross in the summer of 1944. (See page 106.)

Right: Major Heinz Meyer, decorated with the Knight's Cross for his heroic deeds during the battle for Monte Cassino. (See page 111.)

Right: Gallantry above and beyond the call of duty brought Gefreiter Eduard Hug the Knight's Cross of the Iron Cross on 2 September 1944. (See page 113.)

Left: Oberleutnant Wolfgang von Bostell, seen here as a Leutnant, won the Knight's Cross in September 1944 and the Oakleaves in April 1945 (See page 114.)

Above: A highly distinguished officer, Heinrich Keese had his name entered on the Roll of Honour of the German Army on 27 July 1944. (See page 118.)

Above right: Obergefreiter Franz Weber. Note the Close Combat Clasp over his breast pocket signifying participation in hand-to-hand combat. (See page 109.)

Right: Oberleutnant Rudolf Donth. This gallant officer was decorated with the Knight's Cross in 1945 for actions against the British on the Italian Front. (See page 121.)

Above left:
Oberstleutnant Paul Liebing was decorated with the Knight's Cross for his gallantry in the defensive battles on the Western Front in 1945. (See page 125.)

Above:
SS-Sturmbannführer Friedrich Richter was serving with the élite Frundsberg Division when awarded his Knight's Cross in March 1945. (See page 130.)

Left: A former infantryman, SS-Standartenjunker Willi Fey became an accomplished tank commander and went on to serve in the West German army post-war. (See page 128.)

Right: A veteran of the elite Leibstandarte, SS-Obersturmbannführer Gustav-Peter Reber won his Knight's Cross on the Eastern Front in the dying days of the war. (See page 54.)

Right: SS-Sturmbannführer Hans Hauser won the Knight's Cross in May 1945 for his command of a small Kampfgruppe on the Eastern Front. (See page 56.)

ft: The Infantry Assault dge shown here in its ndard silvered form for antry and bronze form motorized infantry.

ttom Left: The General sault Badge shown in numbered patterns for 0 engagements (left) d 50 engagements ght).

ght: The Close Combat asp in Gold, Silver and onze grades. The small ck metal backing plate the centre section is arly seen on the silver de in the centre.

ght: The Tank struction Badge in ld (top) and Silver ttom) grades. The tank dentical on both, only braid differs.

low: The Panzer sault Badge. Shown re are the 75 gagement (left) and 50 gagement (right) tterns.

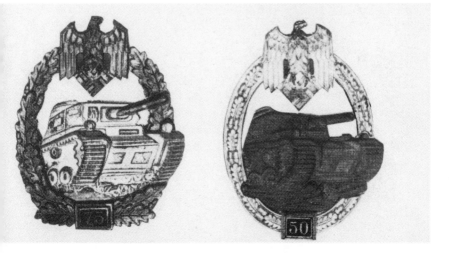

Above: The Luftwaffe Ground Combat Badge (left) shown here with the Luftwaffe paratroopers' qualification badge.

Below: The Knight's Cross of the Iron Cross, an award earned by each of the soldiers covered in this work.

Below: The German Cross in Gold. The term German Cross refers to the large black enamelled swastika in the centre of this badge.

column. Sturm and three of his more experienced men threw themselves into the cover of a drainage ditch and prepared to give battle. 'Sturm, don't fire!,' came the cry from an artillery leutnant who had accompanied Sturm's group, but had now been caught in the open with the bulk of Sturm's boys, helpless in the face of Russian guns. Sturm hesitated. He would rather fight to the end than go into Russian captivity, but he had to think of his boys. If he fired the Russians would respond and they would certainly all die, and did they not deserve every chance to survive?

Sturm threw out his weapon and stood slowly, his hands raised. A group of Russian soldiers ran over to take him prisoner and one spotted his Knight's Cross, which, in broken German, he insisted Sturm remove. Fearing that some of his captors might take his high award as evidence of committed Nazism and treat him accordingly, he quickly removed it and handed it over. Shortly afterwards, Sturm was called over by a Russian major who, he could see, was holding his Knight's Cross. The Russian held out his hand, indicating that Sturm should take back his Cross and put it on. Sturm, understandably, hesitated; did they wish him to display the Knight's Cross at his neck so they could shoot him as an example to the others? Sturm replaced the Knight's Cross, and to his astonishment the major came to attention, lifted his hand to his cap and saluted him. Sturm gladly returned the salute. He had been fortunate enough to be captured by a first-class fighting unit of the Red Army commanded by a chivalrous major who obviously appreciated the status of the Knight's Cross as a symbol of gallantry. Sturm was then put on a truck with the other prisoners, his 'protection' by the Russian major saving him from the souvenir hunting Russian soldiers who were happily robbing his comrades of any valuables. This respite was temporary, and as he passed back through enemy territory towards captivity, other Russians soon looted all his hard-won decorations.

Sturm languished as a prisoner in central Russia for eight long years before he was finally released in October 1953. On returning home, he met his son, now eight years old, for the first time. He had been born in July 1945 shortly after Sturm was captured. Sturm's wife had waited these eight long years for her husband and in November 1954 their marriage was further blessed by the arrival of twin daughters.

In 1954, Hans Sturm returned to a career in engineering with the firm of Rheinstahl Union Brückenbau AG, finally retiring in 1979. He still lives in his native Dortmund.

Leutnant Bruno Sassen

Bruno Sassen was born in Nüttermoor in Ostfriesland on 13 March 1918, the son of a farmer. He took his school leaving certificate in February 1937 at the age of 18 and shortly afterwards, in April, joined the Reichsarbeitsdienst for the usual 6-month period of compulsory labour service. On completion of this Sassen enlisted in the army, joining 2 Kompanie of Kavallerie Regiment 13 in Lüneburg. With this unit he served during the occupation of the Sudetenland in October 1938 with the rank of Gefreiter. By November of that year, Sassen had shown sufficient interest in the care of the unit's animals to be promoted to Unteroffizier and selected for a course at the Veterinary Academy in Hanover as an Officer Aspirant.

At the end of March 1939, Sassen's military service ended to allow him to undertake a course in the study of Animal Medicine at the Hanover Veterinary High School. He was, however, recalled to the colours in September 1939 following the outbreak of war, but continued his studies at the Army Veterinary Academy, passing the first stage of his qualifications in early 1940.

In July 1940, Sassen transferred into the Fallschirmjäger, joining the Paratroop School in Stendal where he underwent his basic training and completed the required number of obligatory jumps to qualify for the Fallschirmschützenabzeichen. Posted to 10 Kompanie of Fallschirmjäger Regiment 3, Sassen was based in Goslar, then Magdeburg, undergoing extensive and very tough combat training in numerous exercise areas.

By May 1941, Sassen held the rank of Oberjäger, a senior private, and on the 20th of that month was a member of the first wave of Fallschirmjäger to be dropped on the Allied-held island of Crete. This first wave comprised the Luftlande Sturm Regiment under General-major Meindl, supported by Fallschirmjäger Regiment 3 under Oberst Heidrich. The main objective for this force was the airfield at Maleme plus a number of key roads and bridges in the Canea region. Fallschirmjäger Regiment 3 had the specific objectives of capturing Galatas, Canea and Suda Bay. The strength of the defending New Zealand troops had been grossly underestimated and Sassen and his comrades found themselves in the thick of ferocious fighting. Sassen's group had some initial success, attacking an enemy tented encampment and taking several prisoners before Sassen himself was wounded in the fighting which raged back and forwards that day, and taken prisoner. Sassen was a prisoner of the New Zealanders for seven days, suffering several bombing attacks on his captors by the Luftwaffe's Stuka dive-bombers before finally being freed after an attack by his own comrades.

Oberjäger Sassen was decorated with the Iron Cross Second Class on 16 June 1941 and the First Class on 28 August 1941, both awards being for his determination and bravery in the face of the enemy in the battle for Crete. In addition, as an active participant in the battle, he qualified for the Kreta Cuffband when this campaign award was introduced in October 1942. It is also interesting to note that Sassen was made an honorary member of the New Zealand Crete Veterans' Association after the war, a mark of the high respect in which these tough German paras were held by their former enemies.

Much depleted by the high losses of the Crete battles, Fallschirm-jäger Regiment 3 and its parent unit, 7th Flieger Division were rebuilt and in the autumn of 1941 transferred to the Eastern Front. Although the Crete battle had been a victory, losses had been so high that Hitler prohibited any further large-scale parachute drops and the German paras were thereafter mostly utilized as infantry. On the opening of the assault on the Soviet Union, Operation 'Barbarossa', German units on the northern sector of the front had made rapid progress. Army Group North, commanded by Generalfeldmarschall Leeb had pushed some of its units over the River Luga within 60 miles of Leningrad by mid July. German hesitation and worry over the security of their supply lines, however, allowed the Russian defenders precious time to prepare the city's defences. Nevertheless, by 1 September Leeb's troops were only seven-and-a-half miles from the city and German shells were falling on Leningrad itself. At this critical stage, Hitler changed his mind and drew forces away from the area to reinforce the drive to Moscow. Leningrad was besieged, but the Germans no longer had the over-whelming weight of numbers required to overrun the city.

It was into this situation that Fallschirmjäger Regiment 3 found itself committed. Sassen and his group were located on the Newa bridgehead near Wyborgskaja in trenches, some of which were only 20 to 30 metres from enemy positions, with specific instructions that the positions be held to the last man. Encouraged by the withdrawal of German forces from this sector of the front, Russian probing attacks began to hit Sassen's positions and for 33 days and nights the beleagured Germans repulsed the enemy probes. On the night of 16 November 1941, enemy troops infiltrated to within four metres of the German positions. Realizing the danger, with a force of just five men Sassen immediately sprang into the attack. Storming into the startled Russian attackers with their machine pistols blazing, Sassen's men succeeded in driving back the enemy and even took some prisoners. Not for the first time a tiny handful of German soldiers led by a determined and fearless soldier, had so startled a much larger group of enemy, that they had lost their nerve and run. Those who escaped had obviously reported the ferocity of the German reaction to their comrades for the next day a large number of demoralized Soviet soldiers deserted and surrendered to the Germans. Sassen's actions were paying high dividends. The Russian intent, to force a breakout through the German positions, was completely foiled.

On the same evening Sassen was given a field promotion to Feldwebel for his actions and was later personally commended by the divisional commander in a special Order of the Day for his gallantry. A recommendation for the Knight's Cross quickly followed as the significance of Sassen's actions became clear. For extreme gallantry in the face of the enemy, Sassen received the Knight's Cross on 22 February 1942.

In April 1942, Sassen attended a 3-month officer candidate course at the Luftwaffe Kriegsschule at Gatow in Berlin, which he successfully passed. He then spent some months in France on occupation duty and intensive training before the regiment once again entrained for the Eastern Front. On 1 October 1942, Sassen was commissioned as a Leutnant.

Serving now on the central sector of the Eastern Front, Leutnant Sassen saw much fierce combat culminating on the night of 25 March 1943. As a platoon commander in 10 Kompanie he led an assault on Russian-held positions east of Twerdy. This important position had been held by the Germans until just one week before when it had been taken by the Russians. Three assault groups were involved in the attack which succeeded in recapturing the position from the enemy after bitter fighting. The enemy, however, launched an immediate counter-attack in great strength and the fighting raged long and hard. On 27 March after two solid days of non-stop combat, a hand-grenade exploded close to Sassen, who was seriously wounded, his foot being smashed. His wounds were so serious that his entire lower left leg had to be amputated. His active combat career was over, but he had the honour of being awarded the German Cross in Gold in recognition of his part in the attack and his personal gallantry in combat. After treatment in various hospitals Sassen was released on home leave. From early 1944, Leutnant Sassen was given several non-combatant home front postings. On 13 February 1945, he was appointed to command a training camp in Military District XI (Hanover) and on 1 April 1945 he was posted to the staff of the military command in his home area of Ostfriesland where he ended the war.

After the war Bruno Sassen returned to his family trade as a farmer, on land leased from his brother. In November 1950, however, he decided to return to the Veterinary Academy in Hanover to complete his veterinary qualifications. With only his disablement pension from the Army, Sassen took on work as a carpenter's assistant to help support his family while he completed his studies. In early

1953, he passed his state examinations and in the summer of that year became a Doctor of Veterinary Medicine, opening a practice in north Ostfriesland. His disablement finally forced his early retirement in 1966.

1943

The disastrous winter losses of 1942 carried over into early 1943. The Russians pushed westward on the south of the front, re-entering the Caucasus. In late January the remnant of Sixth Army surrendered at Stalingrad. February saw the loss of Kharkov and March the loss of Demjansk. Although a German counter-attack took Kharkov back once again, it was but a temporary respite. During the spring, both sides rested as the thaw turned the frozen wastes into an equally inhospitable sea of mud.

In North Africa, Rommel was faring little better. Each German counter-attack only achieved temporary respite as German losses could not be replaced, while the Allies quickly recovered their strength to take the initiative again. In March the British broke through Rommel's Mareth Line defences pushing the Afrika Korps back to Wadi Akarit by early April. Although a small number of German troops escaped to Sicily, the bulk of the Afrika Korps went into captivity in early May. Even the finest German troops could not hold out for ever against overwhelming odds.

Back on the Russian Front, in June Hitler launched Operation 'Zitadelle', the massive armoured offensive on the Kursk salient. One million German soldiers and well over two thousand tanks were launched at the Russian defenders. The enemy were well warned of the attack by their excellent Intelligence and despite making good initial progress, the Germans were halted by a counter-offensive launched at Orel. By mid July the offensive was called off. Vast numbers of irreplaceable tanks had been squandered in this ill-fated offensive. Orel, Bjelgorod and Kharkov all fell to the Russians in August as the Wehrmacht reeled under the hammer blows of the Russian offensive.

The Western Allies were also on the offensive and chased the Germans out of Sicily and on to the Italian mainland. Facing overwhelming odds, Generalfeldmarschall Kesselring's forces fought a masterly retreat up the 'leg' of the Italian mainland to the well-prepared Gustav Line defences. Allied losses were heavy, and progress slow.

Some 1,398 Knight's Crosses and 187 Oakleaves were awarded during 1943, reaching a peak in August with 165 Knight's Cross awards being made in this month.

Oberst Martin Steglich

Martin Steglich was born in Breslau on 16 July 1915. At the age of 21, he began his military career when he joined Fusilier Regiment 12, part of 12th (mecklenburgische) Infanterie Division, in the Baltic seaport of Rostock. By the spring of 1939, having successfully undergone his officer training, he was commissioned Leutnant. Within three days of the outbreak of war, he was made a company commander.

The 12th Infanterie Division served in almost every campaign during the war, beginning with the Polish Campaign where, under the command of General Ludwig von der Leyen, it acquitted itself well, in the drive towards Warsaw. Steglich was awarded the Iron Cross Second Class on 12 September for his part in the division's successful advance.

Following the Polish Campaign, 12th Infanterie Division moved west and in May 1940 as part of Fourth Army, took part in the invasion of France. Once again the division fought well, beating back a French attempt to cut through the extended German Panzer corridor in an attempt to relieve the bulk of the French and British armies which had withdrawn northwards into Belgium. On 27 July, Leutnant Steglich was awarded the Iron Cross First Class for his gallantry and qualities of leadership during the French Campaign. Shortly after the conclusion of the campaign, Steglich was also awarded the Infantry Assault Badge.

In the summer of 1941, 12th Infanterie Division took part in the invasion of the Soviet Union, as part of Sixteenth Army in Heeresgruppe Nord, taking part in the capture of Dvinsk. On 13 July Steglich was awarded the Wound Badge in Black after being wounded in action for the first time. On 1 October 1941, he was promoted to Oberleutnant.

During 1942, the German II Corps had been cut off and encircled by Russian forces near Demjansk. A relief force was assembled, of which 12th Infanterie Division was the major component. After fierce and difficult fighting, the relief force finally broke through to their beleaguered comrades. For his part in the successful relief attempt, Oberleutnant Steglich was decorated with the German Cross in Gold. On 29 July 1942, Oberleutnant Steglich received the East Front Campaign Medal. In December 1942, he was in command of I Kompanie, Grenadier Regiment 89, attached to 123rd Infanterie Division when a powerful Russian attack on his positions near Zemena brought about an action which was to win him great glory. As an illustration of how such actions brought about the award of the Knight's Cross the action is recalled here by a full translation of the original recommendation taken from the original document which is extant.

'Recommendation Nr 1463 for the award of the Knight's Cross of the Iron Cross.

On 23 December 1942 at 10.30 hours, Oberleutnant Steglich received a message that the Russians, in unknown strength, had broken through the neighbouring battalion. Several positions in the front line had been cleared and the anti-tank guns knocked out. All telegraphic connections between the neighbouring units and the Regiment had been shot away. Enemy jamming of the radio also prevented communication by this method.

Oberleutnant Steglich, completely on his own initiative, determined, with all available means to clear out the enemy intrusion into the neighbouring sector and somehow re-establish contact with the rear and with the supporting artillery.

Quickly the assembled assault group set off on the march. Meanwhile the message arrived that the enemy was attacking the command post of the neighbouring Bataillon. The Bataillon commander and his messengers and clerks were engaged in hand-to-hand combat with the enemy. Now there was no possibility of further communications and only by the independent intervention of Oberleutnant Steglich, could there be any chance of halting the breakthrough and destroying the enemy.

But the Russian attack did not slacken. Steglich was indefatigable in his efforts to bring order out of chaos and strengthen the defences in the badly shot-up and burnt front line positions. The enemy probed ever nearer, supported by thundering artillery salvoes. With no thought of rest, Steglich, with unshakeable calm and composure, set a great example to his tired troops, worn out after weeks of continuous combat. Hardly had the night passed, when he realized by the sudden increase in the intensity of the Russian artillery barrage, that the enemy was about to make a further attempt at any cost, to throw the Germans out of their positions and press on with their breakthrough.

At 10.00 hours on 24 December, Steglich was advised that a direct hit on the command post of Hauptmann Buehne had been observed. Buehne, the commander of the neighbouring Bataillon, was dead. Steglich immediately assumed responsibility for the sector and moved his own command post to the command post of his neighbour to ensure better control. By the forenoon, Steglich had made all the preparation he could to defend against the enemy assault. By early evening, however, things looked very serious as a large number of tanks had appeared and were shelling the front-line positions into rubble. Wild defeatist rumours started which Steglich quickly quelled with both encouragements and threats of disciplinary actions.

After heavy casualties by the evening one position was in enemy hands. All through the night the bitter struggle continued, after all available anti-tank weapons had been used up. Meanwhile Rittmeister Besler had the anti-tank defence in hand and in the early morning of 25 December managed to bring up a heavy anti-tank gun. With his defences now more secure, Steglich was ready to launch a counter-attack. With loud cheers, Oberleutnant Steglich stormed forward at the head of his men and closed the gap between the two units.

His heroic bravery and acceptance of responsibility, witnessed by his decisive actions in knocking out the enemy tanks and succeeding in the counter-attack, secured the front line in his own hands. At the crucial moment Steglich was completely on his own. Only thanks to Steglich were communications established between Division and the Artillery commander.

A two-day-long severe crisis through the continued loss of a Bataillon staff in a crucial situation was resolved through the independent determination of Oberleutnant Steglich.

signed. von Mayer
Oberst und Regiments Kommandeur'

'123 Infanterie Division.
Oberleutnant Steglich has displayed special willingness to accept responsibility and outstanding bravery in a crucial situation. Through his personal swift grasp of the situation and his excellent communications between the Division and the Artillery a dangerous Russian breakthrough in the Zemena sector was frustrated.

signed. Rauch
Generalleutnant und Divisions Kdr.
123 Infanterie Division'

'II Armee Korps
Oberleutnant Steglich grasped the personal determination, that after he had heard that Hauptmann Buehne, commander of the neighbouring sector had fallen, to take responsibility for the sector and organize the defence against the continuous heavy enemy attacks. Only the exceptional bravery of this already proven officer is to be thanked that the breakthrough was halted. I advocate the award of the Knight's Cross of the Iron Cross to this proven Officer.

The Commanding General
signed. Laux
General der Infanterie'

'16 Armee
The recommendation for the award of the Knight's Cross of the Iron Cross to Oberleutnant Steglich, Commander of I/Grenadier Regiment 89 is advocated. Oberleutnant Steglich has, through his exceptional personal bravery, his independent resolution and through his energetic leadership, prevented a breakthrough of the enemy to the supply route of the II Armeekorps near Zemena.

Der Oberbefehlshaber
signed Busch
Generaloberst'

'Heeresgruppe Nord   17 January 1943
I advocate this recommendation.
Willingness to accept responsibility and strength of determination in critical situations, great bravery and clear leadership of his troops in the Russian attack against Zemena caused Oberleutnant Steglich to seem fully worthy of the high distinction of the Ritterkreuz.

Der Oberbefehlshaber
signed. von Küchler
Generalfeldmarschall'

The award of the Knight's Cross was finally approved by Hitler on 25 January 1943. A full colonel, three generals and a field marshal had read and approved the recommendation before passing it to the *Heerespersonalamt* (Army Personnel Office) where it would be signed and approved by a staff general before going to Hitler for final authority. So, it can be seen that the awarding of a Knight's Cross was no simple matter and not something to be treated lightly. Although referred to throughout as an Oberleutnant, Steglich had in fact been promoted to Hauptmann on 1 January 1943, after the action referred to but before the recommendation.

On 4 May 1944 Hauptmann Steglich was awarded the Demjansk Shield and the Close Combat Clasp in Bronze. After receiving his award, Steglich attended a course for battalion commanders in Antwerp followed by training as a staff officer and as a regimental commander. He was promoted to Major on 20 April 1944.

In November 1944, Major Steglich became a regimental commander in 180 Infanterie Division, commanding 1221 Infanterie Regiment. The regiment fought in the Venlo area from December 1944 through to January 1945, retreating into Germany as the British pursued them. During the battle for Wesel Major Steglich was again wounded in action, qualifying for the Wound Badge in Silver on 29 March, just after his promotion to Oberstleutnant. The division was decimated at the end of March during Operation 'Varsity', an Allied combined forces offensive using both ground and airborne troops. Its morale badly battered, the division withdrew into the Ruhr. During these difficult months once again Steglich's own personal untiring dedication and personal example was of inestimable value in keeping the spirit of his men from collapsing. This was reflected in the award of the Oakleaves to his Knight's Cross on 5 April 1945. On the cessation of hostilities Steglich was taken prisoner by the Americans but was released in August 1945.

This was by no means the end of Steglich's military career. He rejoined the army when the West German Bundeswehr was formed, being promoted to Oberst on 1 August 1962. Awarded the Order of Merit of the Federal Republic of Germany both Second and First Classes, he is now retired and holds the position of chairman in the Knight's Cross Bearer's Association, the *Ordensgemeinschaft der Ritterkreuztrager*.

Hauptmann Gerd Mischke

Gerd Paul Ludwig Mischke was born in Barmen near Düsseldorf on 16 March 1920. At the age of just nineteen he commenced his military service with 3 Kompanie of Flieger Ausbildungs Regiment 82 in Quakenbrücke. Three months later he was transferred to Fliegerhorst Kompanie Langenhagen and served in this airfield garrison for one year, transferred yet again in June 1940, this time to the Flakartillerie. Mischke remained with Reserve Flak Batterie 35 for just one month, however, before transferring to the Fallschirm Flak Abteilung 2, serving as a Gefreiter with 2 Kompanie.

Even the Flak units attached to the paratroops undertook full jump training and during August 1940 he attended a Fallschirmschützen course at Fallschirmschule 1 in Wittstock-Dosse. On completion of this training he was moved to 2 Kompanie, Fallschirm Flak-Maschinengewehr Bataillon in Aschersleben. Gefreiter Mischke was presented with his qualified paratrooper's badge on 20 October 1940.

On 15 March 1941 Mischke was nominated as a potential officer. This feeling on the part of his superiors was fully justified by Mischke during the attack on Crete. He was a gunner on a 20mm Flak gun when his unit was dropped over Crete on 20 May 1941. In fierce combat against enemy troops on landing near Rethymnon and in a German counter-attack against an enemy breakthrough into their lines two days later, Mischke showed considerable determination and pluck in the face of heavy enemy fire. For this he was decorated with the Iron Cross Second Class on 13 June.

After the successful conclusion of the battle for Crete, Mischke found himself transferred to the Russian Front where, with the rank of Unteroffizier, he served at the Petruschino bridgehead over the River Newa where once again he distinguished himself as gunner with the 20mm Flak. On 28 June 1941 he was decorated with the Iron Cross First Class for these actions. Mischke continued to serve on the Russian Front for the remainder of 1941, seeing much fierce combat on the Newa.

On 18 January 1942, Mischke was sent on an officers' training course at the Luftwaffe Kriegsschule at Berlin–Gatow. During the course of this training he was promoted to Feldwebel and shortly after its completion he was further promoted, to Oberfeldwebel. Mischke's commission finally came on 19 June 1942, when he became a Leutnant der Reserve. Shortly afterwards he was appointed as a platoon commander with 2 Kompanie, Fallschirm Flak Maschinengewehr Bataillon.

In the autumn of 1942, the cancellation of the proposed air assault on Malta released the troops that had been earmarked for this operation, among them a Fallschirmjäger Brigade. This was now dispatched to Egypt to bolster Rommel's Afrika Korps, badly battered by the British offensive at El Alemein. Fallschirmjäger were also committed to the battle for Tunisia. Among the paratroops who served here were an *ad hoc* regiment formed by Oberst Walther Barenthin. Part of this regiment was Fallschirm Panzer Jäger Abteilung 2, in the regiment's III Bataillon. At this time Leutnant Mischke was commander of 1 Kompanie of the Abteilung.

On 26 November, Mischke took part in the formation of a defensive bridgehead between Tunis and Bizerta, where, around Mateur, his company halted an advance towards the north by American tank units. The Barenthin Regiment was attached to the division commanded by General von Manteuffel and during March, took part in an attack on the Jefna positions. Leutnant Mischke and his company served with distinction during this attack, pushing forward relentlessly, knocking out enemy tanks from distances as short as 50 metres. As the enemy counter-attacked, Mischke formed his anti-tank defences, all the while under heavy artillery fire in the sector north of Abjod, proving once again his cool-headed dependability under fire in critical situations.

Much of the action which Mischke saw developed into close-quarter combat, with Allied and German soldiers fighting with small arms, trench knives, entrenching tools and any other weapon available. In defensive battles around Hill 402 and many other strategic positions, Mischke distinguished himself as a gallant and pugnacious soldier. The determined and spirited defence put up by his company in these many actions were not without cost however. By 5 May, the company had only four guns left – 50mm anti-tank cannon. On that day, Mischke and his men thwarted an enemy breakthrough near Sidi Abdallah. The Allies had attempted to break through the left flank of Panzer Grenadier Regiment 160, with armoured support. Protecting the flank of their neighbours, Mischke's company rapidly took the steam out of the Allied attack by knocking out six of the supporting tanks within a short time. The enemy were determined, however, and in the dawn of the following morning once again attempted to push through at the same spot. Mischke destroyed a further eight tanks, once again thwarting the attack. As well as halting the push, Mischke's actions had created an opportunity for the Germans to counter-attack and delay a rapid Allied advance along the main road from Mateur to Tunis.

Leutnant Mischke had shown repeated personal gallantry in fierce combat against a vastly superior enemy force. He was recommended for the Knight's Cross of the Iron Cross and this was awarded on 18 May 1943. During his period of service in North Africa, Mischke had also been awarded his Kreta Cuffband for his part in the successful battle for Crete, and had been awarded the Italo–German Commemorative Medal for the Campaign in Africa. The regiment had occupied a sector of the front sandwiched between two Italian divisions. When the Germans were finally forced to retreat, lack of fuel and transport meant that these units had to be abandoned to their fate. The Italians surrendered, but the Fallschirmjäger were made of sterner stuff. Executing a brilliant ambush of a British column, the paras captured the vehicles and managed to rejoin the remnant of the retreating Afrika Korps. The Fallschirmjäger were evacuated before the final surrender.

The Brigade was used as the nucleus for a new unit, 2 Fallschirm Division. The division was initially stationed in Brittany and fought against the Allied invasion forces in Normandy, taking part in the defence of Brittany, against massive American forces until September. In that month Mischke was promoted to Hauptmann.

Reformed in Germany, 2 Fallschirm Division fought in Holland, and subsequently in the defensive battles against the advancing British up to the crossing of the Rhine. On 1 January 1945, Hauptmann Mischke was awarded the German Cross in Gold for his part in these battles. The division finally surrendered in the Ruhr pocket in March 1945.

Leutnant Wilhelm Wegener

Wilhelm Wegener was born in Seefeld on 21 October 1914. His distinguished military career began on 1 October 1934 when he volunteered for military service and was enlisted into 'V' Batterie, Artillerie Regiment Schwerin, in Perleberg. On 1 May 1939 Wegener, by now an Unteroffizier, attended the Aufklärungs Fliegerschule Brandenburg where he was trained as an aerial artillery spotter. On completion of this specialized training he was posted to the Ersatz Abteilung of Artillery Regiment 48 in Güstrow.

On 8 October 1939, Wegener was sent on a training course for conversion to assault artillery when he attended the Artillerie Lehr Regiment in Jüterbog, to be schooled in the use of the Sturmgeschütz, training which he was soon to put to devastating effect. On completing this training he joined Sturmgeschütz Batterie 640 and served with this unit during the attack on France, winning the Iron Cross Second Class on 3 July 1940. During the French Campaign, Wegener was transferred to the élite Infanterie Regiment (mot.) Grossdeutschland. He was also promoted to the rank of Wachtmeister, a traditional rank of cavalry and mounted personnel commonly carried over into armoured units. It was equivalent to the rank of Feldwebel (sergeant).

After the successful completion of the campaign in France, Grossdeutschland was strengthened and re-equipped to take part in the proposed invasion of Great Britain, and on the cancellation of this operation, was moved east where it took part in the occupation of Belgrade in April 1941. In mid June the regiment moved into the area to the south-east of Warsaw as part of the reserve of 2 Panzerarmee.

On the invasion of the Soviet Union on 21 June 1941, Wegener and his Sturmgeschützen attacked with the rest of the regiment from a launch point just north of Brest–Litovsk. In late March and into early April, the regiment took part in heavy fighting against Red Army units near Minsk, following the retreating Russians in a series of continuous minor skirmishes all the way up to and across the River Dnieper. From its crossing point between Orsha and Mogilev, the regiment moved north-east to take part in furious combat around Yelnya in mid July. During this latter action, Wegener was decorated with the Iron Cross First Class.

Moving south, Grossdeutschland saw further fierce action around Vaskovo during the latter half of August, Wegener being wounded in action for the first time during these battles. Continuing its move southwards, the regiment hit Russian resistance again at Konotop in early September and forced its way south in continual action against the enemy, reaching Romny at the end of the month. Grossdeutschland successfully resisted desperate counter-attacks in the Romny area in late September and early October.

This élite regiment was then transported north where it took part in the defeat of the Russian forces at Bryansk. After a few days rest and recuperation in this area, Grossdeutschland was thrown into action again in the area around Tula, to the south of Moscow. In the muddy conditions which preceded the full horrors of the Russian winter the regiment attempted to bypass Tula to the east and attack the city from the north. Russian resistance was stiffening considerably as the Germans neared Moscow, however, and the regiment suffered considerable casualties during this action. On 30 November 1941, Wegener was promoted to Oberwachtmeister. Grossdeutschland units then moved slightly further south into the area around Bolkhov where the remainder of the year was spent in defensive actions against furious Russian counter-attacks. The regiment's first six months of action on the Russian Front brought it a considerable reputation as a high-grade combat unit. This was only achieved, however, at the cost of heavy casualties, with more than 4,000 men killed, wounded or missing in action.

In January 1942, Grossdeutschland was involved in combat against Red Army and partisan units around Gorodok and the battle to secure the vital Bolkhov to Yagodnaya railway, suffering heavy losses once again. By the spring the area had been secured and the opportunity was taken to remove the regiment from the front and rebuild the battered unit. The regiment was expanded to become Infanterie Division (mot.) Grossdeutschland. Brought up to full strength and issued with the finest of arms and equipment, the men had proven themselves worthy of their élite status.

By late June Grossdeutschland was ready to return to action, and on the 28th of the month it crossed the River Tim and broke through the Russian positions, pursuing the fleeing enemy all the way to Voronezh. Turning south, the division made a rapid advance to the River Donetz at its junction with the Don. In early August the division was transported by rail to Smolensk in preparation for the defence of Rzhev against impending Russian attack. Grossdeutschland would remain in this area until January 1943, seeing some of the fiercest combat it had experienced so far, and suffering from the horrendous weather. It had been a difficult year for the division. Its élite status had led high command to overestimate its abilities and expect too much of it. Hence casualties were heavy with losses of more than 10,000 officers and men. Those who survived, however, were now hardened veterans.

After the front at Rshew had been secured, Grossdeutschland moved south to Smolensk where it entrained for Volchansk, near Byelgorod. Here it went into action against powerful Red Army forces east of Byelgorod where, despite their best efforts, the Germans were pushed back, losing Byelgorod to the enemy on 8 February and Kharkov on 15 February. The division was pulled back to the area south of Poltava where it was reinforced with the addition of a company of powerful Tiger tanks in preparation for a counter-attack. This began in early March and Grossdeutschland units captured Bogodukhov on 11 March and Tomarovka on 19 March. On 23 March the division was once again withdrawn to receive new weapons and equipment. In June, just prior to Operation 'Zitadelle', the attack on the Kursk salient, the division was upgraded from an Infanterie to a Panzer Grenadier Division. On 13 June 1943, Oberwachtmeister Wegener was decorated with the Knight's Cross of the Iron Cross for actions during the counter-attack on Kharkov.

In combat near Scherustow and Iskrowka, after the lead Sturm-geschütz of his company had been put out of action, Wegener had taken the initiative and determined to recapture both of these towns from the Russians. His resolute personal action, without regard for his personal safety, was responsible for the destruction of three 122mm howitzers, one 76mm and two 47mm anti-tank positions. At Alexand-rowka he had further distinguished himself by knocking out four enemy tanks, two 122mm guns, eight 76mm and six 47mm anti-tank guns. His exemplary personal gallantry and his daring determination had a decisive effect on the battle, contributing in no small way to the victory.

Wegener's greatest achievement, however, came during the action at Stanowje. Here the Sturmgeschützen from Grossdeutschland ran into a powerful force of Russian tanks. As the Sturmgeschützen gave battle to the approaching enemy, Wegener manoeuvred himself around to the enemy flanks, and oblivious of the overwhelming numerical superiority of the Russians, immediately went into the attack. Twelve enemy tanks fell victim to Wegener's gun. Wegener fired until his last shell was gone, then withdrew, refuelled and replenished his ammunition and went straight back into action, taking on up to forty enemy tanks in furious combat until the Sturmgeschützen were relieved by a company of Tiger tanks in the evening. The division was extremely proud of this young daredevil who had shown utter contempt of the danger in which he stood and was ready to take on an overwhelmingly superior enemy.

Grossdeutschland took part in the ill-fated offensive Operation 'Zitadelle'. The division made reasonable progress in the early stages and despite strong defences in Grossdeutschland's sector, finally broke through the enemy lines, but with heavy casualties. On 17 July the divsion was relieved and pulled south to Tomarovka. After a few days' rest it was moved once again, attached to Heeresgruppe Mitte around Karachev where it defended against Russian forces attacking from the Bolkhov region.

At the beginning of August the division was moved yet again, this time to the southern sector of the front near Akhturkha where it received a full Abteilung of Tiger tanks. Thus reinforced it went into action again at Akhturkha. Grossdeutschland became a 'fire-brigade', being rushed from place to place all over the front wherever the situation looked most critical. This was one of the great disadvantages of being an élite unit with a formidable fighting reputation. The division was always where the fighting was at its toughest, and suffered commensurately heavy casualties. The Waffen-SS counterpart, the élite Leibstandarte, suffered from similar problems. In September, Grossdeutschland took part in the defence of the River Dnieper before being withdrawn to France for a complete refit. This was much needed as at one point the entire division could boast only one tank!

At the beginning of October Grossdeutschland was back at the Dnieper, but this time in the attack, as the Germans pushed back over the river and threw the enemy back. Within a couple of weeks, however, the Russians had launched yet another offensive and the division was engaged in defensive battles east of Krivoi-Rog. The following year was just as difficult, with defensive battles at Kirovograd, Targul Frumos and on the northern sector of the front in the defence of the Memel bridgehead. Although Grossdeutschland did launch successful counter-attacks at Targul Frumos, Podul and Virballen, these were of only temporary benefit. Even the superhuman efforts of the Wehrmacht's most élite divisions could only delay and not halt the inexorable advance of the massive Russian war machine.

In August 1944, Wegener was selected for officer training and in October attended the Kriegsschule in Munich. On completion of this course he was commissioned Leutnant. He returned to 3 Batterie, Sturmgeschütz Brigade Grossdeutschland at the end of November, and took part in the defence of the port of Memel, being evacuated just before Memel fell to the enemy. The division was moved to Rastenburg where once again it was expanded, now becoming a Panzer Korps. The brigades attached to Grossdeutschland such as the Führerbegleit Brigade and the Führer Grenadier Brigade were expanded to divisional strength in their own right.

In mid-January, Grossdeutschland was thrown back into the line to keep open the Orzyk bridgehead. The division gradually retreated through northern Poland into East Prussia, to the area around Königsberg. Here, in the most savage defensive battles against the Red Army, Wegener was seriously wounded and had to be evacuated for treatment. He spent the next few months recovering in various hospitals in Germany. Eventually he was taken prisoner by the British before being released in July 1945.

SS-Unterscharführer Remi Schrynen

Remi Schrynen was born in Kumtich, in Flanders, Belgium on 24 December 1921. In 1942, as a young idealist with strong anti-Communist feelings, he volunteered for service with the German Army in the east in the so-called 'European Crusade against Bolshevism'. The German propagandists had been highly successful in recruiting west-European volunteers. Young men from France, Belgium, Holland, Norway, Denmark, Finland and even a handful from Great Britain served in the field grey of the army or Waffen-SS. Some were turncoat prisoners of war, some were crass opportunists who did little more than kowtow to the Germans when they were victorious and rapidly desert when the tide turned. Most, however, were young and misguided idealists who genuinely were taken in by the idea of a new European Order.

The 21-year-old Schrynen found himself as a company runner in the SS-Freiwilligen Legion Flandern in 1942. Going into action for the first time at the end of May 1943, Schrynen served on the northern sector of the Russian Front near Leningrad. Later that month the Legion was rearranged as SS-Sturmbrigade Langemarck, and Schrynen became a gunner in 3 (Panzerjäger) Kompanie, where he served on a powerful high-velocity 75mm anti-tank gun. At the end of 1943, the brigade was on the southern sector of the front around Kiev. On 31 December Schrynen, either with 3 Platoon or the company, personally knocked out three T-34 tanks during a powerful Russian massed infantry attack with armoured support. Schrynen had shown himself to be a proficient and dependable soldier who could keep his head in critical situations. He had been wounded in action seven times in little more than a year, indicating the ferocity of the combat in which he had taken part.

SS-Sturmmann Schrynen, however, was to show himself not just as a proficient soldier but as a man of exceptional personal gallantry during an action in June 1944. He was one of a special Kampfgruppe composed of volunteers on the northern sector of the front near Narwa. A massive artillery barrage had battered the German positions, and the SS-Grenadiers knew that this was but the forerunner of a powerful attack on the Kampfgruppe's position. The Russians hardly needed to bother with tactical manoeuvring but could overrun the German positions with sheer weight of numbers. No matter how many soldiers were killed, others would take their place until the enemy was overwhelmed. Sure enough, massed Russian infantry were soon approaching the German lines, with powerful armoured support. Schrynen calmly waited at his 75mm cannon until the enemy tanks were well within range, then opened fire. Within a few minutes four T-34s were in flames, with two others disabled. The battle raged on, but eventually numerical superiority began to wear down the Kampf-gruppe. Initially 400 strong, as the days dragged by the numbers were whittled down until only three officers and 35 men were still alive. Schrynen's gun crew had put up a determined defence, knocking out many enemy tanks, but now his crew were all killed or wounded; only Schrynen remained.

The order was given to pull back and the remaining Grenadiers slowly withdrew to the rear. Schrynen, however, was made of sterner stuff. He had heard the order to withdraw but refused. He remained alone, loading, aiming and firing his anti-tank gun. Realizing the Germans were pulling back, the Russians launched yet another massed infantry attack. Schrynen would have no chance of survival. Watching the scene, however, was a radio operator who had been mortally wounded, and left behind when the remnant of the Kampfgruppe withdrew. Knowing he was dying, and with nothing to lose, he called down German artillery fire on his own positions.

The Russian infantry drew nearer and Schrynen could see with them some 30 tanks some of which were of the new heavy Josef Stalin type, the remainder being T-34s. He immediately opened fire and in the dramatic battle which ensued destroyed three Stalin tanks and four T-34s. Then one of the remaining Stalins, from a range of just 30 metres, scored a direct hit on his gun. Schrynen was flung back like a rag doll and severely wounded. Around him lay scattered the burning wreckage of a dozen enemy tanks, knocked out by Schrynen during this ferocious battle. The severely wounded gunner was found by his own troops after a successful armoured counter-attack had thrown back the enemy. He was immediately recommended for the Knight's Cross of the Iron Cross for his extreme heroism. This was approved in due course and after he had recovered from his wounds, Schrynen was decorated with Knight's Cross in front of the entire Brigade, the medal being hung around his neck by the brigade commander, SS-Obersturmbannführer Conrad Schellong. Schrynen also received the Wound Badge in Gold and was promoted to SS-Unterscharführer.

At about the time that Schrynen received his award, the brigade was expanded to divisional status as 27 SS-Freiwilligen Panzer Grenadier Division Langemarck. Schrynen fought with the division in the retreat from Poland and Pomerania and in the battle for Berlin. It is ironic that in the final battle to defend the doomed capital of Nazi Germany many of the young SS-Grenadiers who gave their lives were Belgians, Frenchmen and even a couple of Englishmen from the Britische Freikorps. Remi Schrynen was luckier. He survived this last great conflagration and was taken prisoner.

He was held as a traitor rather than as a prisoner of war, in what he himself has described as a Belgian Concentration Camp where he and other SS-Volunteers were brutally treated. Finally released in January 1955 he moved to West Germany in 1962, disillusioned by the treatment received in his own country. As a reservist with the West German Bundeswehr, Schrynen once again found the soldierly comradeship he had missed so much and made good friends with soldiers from all the Nato armies. He is now retired and lives in Hagen.

SS-Hauptsturmführer Georg Karck

Georg Karck was born in Bad Segeberg in Holstein on 11 June 1911, the son of master glazier Richard Karck. On completion of his education he followed his father into the construction industry and became a glazier.

Like many young Germans during the volatile days of the late twenties and early thirties, Karck found himself attracted by the promise of full employment and renewed national pride offered by the National Socialists. As early as 1930, Karck had joined the SA Stormtroopers. Just one year later he joined the Nazi Party and at the same time enlisted in the SS. From 1933 to 1937, Karck served as a volunteer in the élite Leibstandarte SS Adolf Hitler. During the early days of this most élite of units, prospective candidates greatly outnumbered vacancies and only the very best candidates were accepted. Even such simple imperfections as a single tooth filling could lose a candidate his place, so great was the competition for entry.

After completion of his service with the Leibstandarte, Karck was discharged and returned to his civilian trade as a glazier. In 1938, however, he was recalled for service during the occupation of the Sudetenland, thereafter remaining on the reserve list until being recalled once again on the outbreak of war.

Karck then served as a Platoon Commander during the Western Campaign and during the invasion of Greece, acquiring a reputation for dependability and efficiency. June 1941 found Karck serving with the Leibstandarte's II Bataillon during the invasion of the Soviet Union on the southern sector of the front, through Zhitomir Nikolayev, Taganrog and Rostov, where the Leibstandarte achieved considerable success and considerably enhanced its growing reputation as a first-class combat unit. Karck's fearless attitude during these battles and his fatherly concern for his men earned him their respect and admiration and gained him the Iron Cross Second Class on 20 April 1942.

In August 1942 Karck was promoted to SS-Obersturmführer. The recommendation for this promotion came from his battalion commander, Rudolf Sandig, and was quickly confirmed by the Leibstandarte's charismatic commander, SS-Obergruppenführer Sepp Dietrich. On 25 August 1942 Karck received the East Front Campaign Medal.

Early 1943 found massive battles raging back and forward between the Donetz and the Dnieper. By late February, Taganrog and Rostov had been recaptured by the Russians and even Kharkov was finally lost when SS-Obergruppenführer Paul Hausser, ignoring Hitler's express orders to hold the city, broke out northwards to avoid certain annihilation. Hitler, furious at the loss of Kharkov, pressed for its rapid recapture and once again the Leibstandarte was to play a major part. While XLVIII Panzer Korps forced back the Russian forces, Leibstandarte and Totenkopf Division troops pushed into Kharkov from the north while troops from the Das Reich Division entered from the west. Four days of the most bitter house-to-house fighting ensued before, on 14 March, Kharkov was once again in German hands. For his gallantry in the face of the enemy during this vicious battle, Karck was awarded the Iron Cross First Class on 12 March 1943. During the following month Karck qualified for the Panzerkampfabzeichen in Bronze.

After the Kharkov action, the Leibstandarte was allowed a short period of rest and refitting. Always in the forefront of the fiercest action, it had lost more than 4,500 men during the recapture of Kharkov. The respite for Karck and his men was brief, however, and the Leibstandarte was soon in action again, committed to the ill-fated assault on the Kursk salient, Operation 'Zitadelle', in July 1943. On 4 July, the regiment was given the task of mounting a surprise attack on the Russian defensive positions of Hill 228.6 north-west of Jachostoff, intended to capture the proposed starting-point for the Leibstandarte in the offensive, due to start over a wide front on the following day.

On the night of 4/5 July Karck led his men in an assault on the Russian positions, engaging the desperate defenders in fierce hand-to-hand combat, throughout the twisting trench system. Despite the spirited defence put up by the enemy, Karck spurred his men ever deeper into the enemy positions and led the advance metre by metre towards the top of the hill. Despite receiving a head wound, Karck pressed onwards, personally accounting for five enemy bunkers. The entire Russian strength on the hill was overwhelmed and all were either killed or taken prisoner.

Alarmed at this situation, the Russians threw in an immediate counter-attack resulting once again in bitter hand-to-hand fighting. It was principally through the superb example of selfless gallantry and contempt of personal danger set by Karck to his men that after over two hours' bloody fighting the enemy counter-attack was repulsed with heavy losses and the hill remained in German hands. The launch-point for the offensive was secured. On 5 July the assault began, advancing through deeply entrenched defensive positions protected by minefields and anti-tank ditches. Karck's regiment moved on Bykowka, with him and his men once again in the spearhead position.

Karck soon found himself committed to yet another attack on an enemy-held hill. With only a small hand-picked assault group, Karck was to create a gap in the defensive minefield for the following armour and then throw the defenders back off their positions. Karck pushed his men on to even greater achievements, pursuing the fleeing enemy. His men, now nearing exhaustion, drove themselves after the Russians, preventing them from establishing defensive positions in Bykowka itself. The fact that the regiment achieved all its objectives was in no small measure due to the shining example of personal bravery and fearless determination shown by Karck, and his inspired leadership of his equally brave Grenadiers.

On 23 July 1943 Karck's regimental commander, SS-Obersturm-bannführer Hugo Krass, recommended him for the Knight's Cross of the Iron Cross. This was approved and on 3 August 1943 Karck joined the ranks of the *Ritterkreuzträger*. At about this time Karck was strongly recommended for a well-deserved promotion. The high opinions held of him are well reflected in the comments made in the recommendation by his commander, Rudolf Sandig.

'Karck is straightforward, direct, just and reliable. On the grounds of his long membership of the Leibstandarte, his service both home and overseas has been highly meritorious.

In action, he has proven himself exceptional as a platoon commander on the grounds of his military knowledge and his soldierly attitude. He has been a constant example to his men of what a good SS-Man should be.'

His promotion to SS-Sturmbannführer was approved on 9 November 1943, but in view of his decoration was later backdated to the start of the month following the award of the *Ritterkreuz*, at the specific request of his superiors.

The award of the *Ritterkreuz* usually attracted a welcome spell of home leave. This served a dual purpose, being a reward to the new hero and also a useful propaganda exercise, raising morale on the home front; the returning hero would undoubtedly be fêted by the local populace. So it was with Karck. The people of his home town of Bad Segeberg were naturally proud of his deeds and the local Nazi hierarchy were anxious to extract the maximum propaganda from this hero and a formal reception was arranged. On the day of his homecoming the local Sturmabteilung, Hitlerjugend and Party leadership officials – the Kreisleiter, Ortsgruppenleiter and other 'Golden Pheasants' – arrived at the railway station bedecked in their finest uniforms, while a band played stirring martial music. The next station down the line telephoned to say Karck's train had passed through and should be arriving any time. The hero of the day was about to arrive. Soon the Sturmabteilung band and the guard of honour were ready for the highlight of the day as the train drew alongside the platform and halted, the door to Karck's compartment neatly lined up alongside the posturing Nazi hierarchy. As the crowd thronged forward to glimpse a view of their hero, the waiting dignitaries grew nervous. Where was their hero? As the crowds fidgeted, one of the Party officials sent a guard to fetch Karck off the train. The Reichsbahn employee entered the carriage and immediately reappeared shrugging his shoulders – no Karck! The music faltered and stopped as the train slowly pulled out, leaving the reception committee totally bewildered.

What had happened? Well, despite the fact that Karck had been an early supporter of the Nazis and a Stormtrooper himself, four years' hard combat at the front had changed him from a fanatical idealist to a hard-bitten realist. He was no respecter of these pompous strutting sycophants of the political leadership. As the train drew nearer to Bad Segeberg, Karck had become depressed at the thought of having to listen to their interminable political prattle. As an experienced front-line soldier he had no wish to suffer the patronising attitudes of these desk-bound warriors who had never been near a real battle. When the train reached Sitengörs, the last stop before Bad Segeberg, Karck had slipped away and made his way home over the fields by paths known to him since childhood, and reached his parents' home undisturbed. The embarrassment caused to the party big-wigs was Karck's silent protest on behalf of the front-line soldier and is an interesting illustration that even such a committed SS man was a soldier first and foremost, with barely disguised contempt for the 'politicals'.

Karck's leave was soon over and he returned to his comrades on the Eastern Front. On 8 November 1943, a transport train from 8 and 9 Companies under Karck's command was in Kosanka, west of Fastow, when loud explosions were heard. The enemy had blown up the line and were massing for an attack on the station. Karck quickly organized defensive positions around the perimeters of the station and through the course of the night, repulsed several enemy attacks. At dawn the enemy renewed the assault, this time with tank support. With only small arms available, Karck formed his small force into tank-hunting teams and managed to hold the enemy at bay until a message arrived ordering him to withdraw. Surrounded by enemy forces with up to thirty tanks in support, Karck's small group nevertheless succeeded in breaking out, destroying five enemy tanks in the process. An arduous 80-kilometre forced march followed before the Germans under Karck's leadership reached their own lines, suffering only minimal losses. Karck, despite being wounded, once again had shown his men a prime example of cool-headed leadership.

On 5 March 1944 Karck was tasked to occupy and hold a position north-east of Basaliya. Once esconced in their positions his men came under attack from Russian infantry who had made their approach under cover of a snowstorm. Soon the weakly held German left flank was in danger of being rolled up by the enemy. Karck quickly realized the danger and, checking his available resources, came up with a single Sturmgeschütz assault gun and a motorized 2cm Flak gun. Sitting on the assault gun, he personally led the counter-attack which successfully repulsed the enemy. The Russians lost 240 men killed and 40 were taken prisoner.

Karck's commander at this time, SS-Brigadeführer Preiss, recommended him for the German Cross in Gold in recognition of his deeds. Preiss appended his own personal comment to the recommendation papers:

'Karck has constantly distinguished himself through his pluck and daredevilry. A great example to his men, he has mastered many a dangerous situation through his verve and skill in a crisis. Karck is one of my best Company Commanders. An award of the German Cross in Gold is warmly recommended.'

In the spring of 1944 the Leibstandarte was transferred to the Western Front to bolster the German defences in view of the imminent Allied invasion. The élite Leibstandarte Adolf Hitler was soon in the thick of the fighting and Karck and his men applied themselves with their customary élan. At this time Karck commanded II Bataillon, SS Panzer Grenadier Regiment 2.

On the night of 3 July Karck was travelling in a Volkswagen Kubelwagen jeep towards his unit lines. Being in a front-line area, the vehicle had to travel without headlights. Taking a bend at speed, the Kubelwagen collided with a supply lorry and its fuel tank, which in the Kubelwagen was located just in front of the driver's position, ruptured and burst into flames. The lorry was carrying munitions which immediately exploded and Karck and his driver were killed outright. Karck's proposed German Cross was approved posthumously and he was also posthumously promoted to SS-Sturmbannführer.

In mid February 1945, General Burgdorf of the Oberkommando des Heeres visited Karck's widow Ingeborg and presented her with 5,000 Reichsmarks for each of her three sons, from Hitler's personal funds. In the full knowledge of Karck's gallantry, Hitler wished to ensure that at least the costs of his sons' education would be met.

Whatever Karck's political beliefs, at least in the early days, may have been, his personal heroism is beyond doubt. A soldier's soldier, thoughtful and considerate of his subordinates' welfare but personally indifferent to danger, Karck was sorely missed by his comrades and to this day is remembered with great fondness by his former Waffen-SS comrades. A worthy *Ritterkreuzträger*.

SS-Untersturmführer Alfred Schneidereit

Alfred Schneidereit was born on 29 October 1919 in the town of Insterburg in East Prussia. At the age of 25 he was serving with 8 Kompanie, SS Panzer Grenadier Regiment 1 of the élite Leibstandarte SS Adolf Hitler, with the rank of Rottenführer, a junior corporal.

In late 1943 SS Panzer Grenadier Regiment 1 had been considerably reinforced with tanks, assault guns and artillery and renamed Kampfgruppe Frey after its commander, SS-Obersturmbannführer Albert Frey. Serving on the Eastern Front, the Kampfgruppe was located at the village of Kotscherewo near the Zhitomir–Kiev highway. Under orders to stand fast and hold their positions at any price, these élite young Grenadiers were accustomed to such exhortations. Far from the support of the rest of the division, the Grenadiers knew they were in for a very tough time of it, but were resolute in their determination to fulfil their task. Heavy enemy tank concentrations had been spotted and it was clear that the enemy was preparing to launch an assault. The German supply lines had been cut.

On the eastern edge of the defence lines in the 8 Kompanie position, Rottenführer Schneidereit lay with his bazooka at the ready, awaiting the inevitable appearance of the enemy. At 0600 hours came a furious artillery bombardment to soften-up the German positions prior to a massed infantry assault, accompanied by seemingly endless salvoes from the 'Stalin Organs' (multiple-barrelled rocket-launchers).

The barrage ceased and masses of Russian infantry were soon sighted, supported by T-34 tanks. Schneidereit sprang into action, his bazooka roared and the first T-34 burst into flames. Within thirty minutes he destroyed two T-34s and disabled two more. Around him his comrades with their MG-34 belt-fed machine-guns mowed down seemingly endless numbers of infantry, but always more would take their place. Again the Russians pushed forward, this time reaching the German positions. Schneidereit's company was badly mauled and had to pull back for a hundred metres or so to new positions. In the close-quarter fighting which accompanied this withdrawal, Schneidereit was wounded by grenade shrapnel, but managed to bind the wound himself with his field dressing. Wave after wave of enemy infantry threw themselves at the German positions, seemingly oblivious of their horrendous losses as German machine-gun fire continued to scythe them down. The enemy's supply of manpower, artillery shells and tanks seemed endless. Schneidereit's company commander and many of his comrades were killed.

At midday the Soviets broke through and the company was gradually forced back, enfuriating Schneidereit, who was determined to hold on. Gathering up a few comrades and a machine-gun he stormed forward against the tide of Russian infantry. Eventually, Schneidereit's little group reached his old position, where his bazooka lay undamaged, and once again he opened fire on the enemy. Despite the heroic efforts of the group, the Russian advance was relentless and the outcome of the battle was no longer in any doubt. Artillery and rocket salvoes still bombarded the German positions and Russian infantry swarmed all over the area. By evening the company was worn out. All officers and NCOs were dead and one after another the German machine-gun positions fell silent. Now Schneidereit and his comrades would also have to withdraw. Schneidereit grasped his bazooka and prepared to move back. Immediately the weapon was hit and blown to pieces, and two of the fingers of his left hand were ripped off. A quickly applied field dressing was barely able to staunch the flow of blood as his comrades helped him to the rear.

Unbelievably, an order came through from the Kampfgruppe – the company must hold its positions until the next day without reinforcements. The meagre remnant, barely enough for two infantry sections, huddled in a hollow in the ground, stunned. How could they possibly hold out? As the next wave of Russian assault troops approached, however, Schneidereit once again took the initiative, leaping forward with a machine pistol in his undamaged hand and leading the small German force into a determined counter-attack. Two machine-guns were recovered from the rubble and set up to give covering fire. A defensive position was formed and so ferocious was the German fire that the enemy were fooled into thinking their strength was much greater. These few survivors from 8 Kompanie held the position throughout the night despite many Russian attacks. Relieved the next day, Schneidereit's men helped him to the first-aid post where he collapsed unconscious. As soon as news of his gallantry reached the Kampfgruppe he was recommended for the Knight's Cross of the Iron Cross. This was approved and Schneidereit joined the ranks of the *Ritterkreuztrager* on 20 December 1944. He was also promoted to SS-Unterscharführer.

Schneidereit recovered from his wounds and returned to serve for the rest of the war with the Leibstandarte, eventually taking part in the defence of Berlin where he yet again distinguished himself in action. Eventually being commissioned as an SS-Untersturmführer, Schneidereit was a perfect example of the selfless gallantry often shown by the common German infantry soldier. A mere corporal, he displayed great gallantry and leadership qualities in the direst of situations, inspiring his comrades to ever greater efforts.

Schneidereit survived the war and now lives in retirement.

1944

The start of a new year brought no joy to the troops of the Wehrmacht. In early January the Red Army crossed the Polish border. Soviet territory on the northern sector of the front, won at the cost of so many German lives, had all been lost. Russian troops were also advancing in the south with Kirovograd and Novgorod captured by the Red Army in January. By the spring, the Russians had entered Roumania, and by mid May the entire Crimea was back in Russian hands.

During August the full scale of the disaster on the Russian Front became clear to the German people; Russian shells began to fall on German territory for the first time, when Mariampole in East Prussia was bombarded by Red Army artillery units. The Wehrmacht was still capable of showing its teeth, however, but incidents such as those at Debrecen where a local German counter-attack cut off and destroyed three entire Russian corps were becoming increasingly rare. Hitler's ludicrous 'stand and fight to the last bullet' type strategy cost the Germans dearly in both men and equipment which could have been saved. Although the German war industry was still managing to produce considerable numbers of tanks, aircraft and guns, there were fewer and fewer trained soldiers left alive to use them, or fuel to allow sufficient training.

In Italy, the stout defence put up by the Germans slowed the Allied advance considerably. Situations such as that at Cassino saw hard-pressed German soldiers fighting against overwhelming odds in superb defensive actions which enhanced their fighting reputation considerably. The defenders at Cassino lost some ten thousand men, but the cost to the Allies was forty thousand men to dislodge them. Even then the German defenders withdrew rather than actually suffering defeat.

Even at this stage the Wehrmacht was still powerful enough to have carried on the war for a few years to come, but in June the Allies struck a mortal blow to any hope of survival for the Third Reich when the long-awaited invasion of Europe was launched. Within just six days, despite all the efforts of the German defenders to stop them, the Allies had landed more than 320,000 troops and by the beginning of

July this number had grown to almost one million. Bleeding dry on the Russian Front, pushed ever backwards in Italy, the Wehrmacht was now being severely battered in the west. Overwhelming Allied air superiority meant that what troops were available could only move at night for fear of Allied fighter-bombers. Soon the Western Allies were also at the gates of the Reich, but Hitler had one last desperate gamble to make.

Amazingly, at this late stage in the war, Hitler had managed secretly to assemble a massive and powerful armoured force with which he intended to launch a counter-attack through the Ardennes, split the Allies and drive to the English Channel. Initially the offensive, launched on 16 December, was a total shock to the Allies who reeled back in disarray. With bad weather grounding the Allied air forces, the panzer armies created chaos. As ever, lack of fuel and over-extended lines of communication began to take their toll. The German advance began to founder, and, when improving weather allowed the full weight of Allied air power to be brought to bear, the Germans were stopped well short of their target.

All of these desperately needed and irreplaceable panzer units had once again been squandered for one of Hitler's grandiose schemes. Now the Germans had precious little left in reserve and the end could not be long delayed. The desperate and often heroic defence put up by the crumbling German armies is well attested to by the number of awards made of the Knight's Cross. A total of 2,448 were awarded, together with 326 Oakleaves and 76 Swords. The peak came in October 1944 when 327 Knight's Crosses were awarded in one single month.

Major Günther Hochgarz

Günther Hochgarz began his military career on 1 September 1939 when he was conscripted for military service on the outbreak of war. In the same month, after various physical and psychological tests, he was adjudged as suitable officer material and sent for officer candidate training. In February 1940, Hochgarz joined Infanterie Regiment 187 in 87 Infanterie Division as a machine-gunner. (In 1944 he was to become regimental commander of the same unit.)

In April 1940 Hochgarz was promoted to Gefreiter and appointed section leader. May 1940 found him in action during the invasion of France, undergoing his baptism of fire during the breakthrough at the Weygand Line on the Somme. In Hochgarz's eight-man section, four had been killed and two wounded by the end of one day's combat – testimony to the ferocity of the fighting. On 15 June Hochgarz was one of the first footsoldiers to take part in the victory parade in Paris. July

1940 saw Hochgarz's service during the Battle of France rewarded by promotion to Unteroffizier and the award of the Iron Cross Second Class.

In March 1941 Infanterie Regiment 187 was transferred to West Prussia and on 1 April Hochgarz was promoted to Feldwebel. He took part in the invasion of the Soviet Union in June 1941 as second in command of a machine-gun company, a spearhead unit of the division. During the next few months he saw fierce fighting in several important actions: the capture of Ossowisce Fortress, the Byalistock cauldron, Ossipowitschiand, the Battle for Smolensk, with many classic infantry attacks from village to village, hand-to-hand fighting and fast assault actions. The advance along the route Wiasma–Gshatch–Rusa and the flanking of Swenigerode brought the regiment to just 33 kilometres from Moscow.

On 15 November 1941 Hochgarz was wounded in action for the first time, suffering a bullet wound through his left upper thigh, but returned to action after first-aid treatment. During the following month he suffered his second wound as his unit pulled back from Moscow, being wounded in the thigh by machine-gun fire from a Russian aircraft which was strafing his unit. Once again his wound was not too serious and he was able to remain with the unit. Four days after his second wound he was decorated with the Iron Cross First Class. On 20 March 1942 Feldwebel Hochgarz was once again wounded in action, this time a calf wound caused by a splinter from a hand-grenade during a defensive action against Soviet encroachments into the German positions around Gshatsk.

Having qualified for his Infantry Assault Badge after the requisite number of actions he received the award on 20 March 1942. On 1 April 1942, having proved himself as a private soldier and NCO in combat, his officer candidate training was rewarded by commissioning to the rank of Leutnant and on 1 May, long delayed, he finally received his Black wound badge actually earned with his first wound in November 1941.

In the summer of that year Hochgarz saw action around Beloy before the division was moved to Rshew in July. During this period, having been wounded in the lower right arm, he qualified for the wound badge in silver. This time the wound was serious enough to require hospital treatment and he was evacuated to Germany. Recuperating, he was given his first home leave for fully two years. Just ten days before Christmas, Hochgarz returned to the front and rejoined his regiment, still lying before Rshew.

On 1 March 1943, Hochgarz was promoted to Oberleutnant and three months later qualified for the Close Combat Clasp in Bronze. In July he was wounded for the fifth time, by a splinter from an exploding artillery shell. At this time his regiment was involved in trench warfare near Welish. His wound qualified him for the wound badge in Gold.

A fairly quiet period of three or four weeks ended when an attack by T-34 tanks was made on the divisional area. Hochgarz organized his men into tank-hunting teams and he himself succeeded in destroying a T-34 with a magnetic charge, earning himself his first *Panzervernichtungsabzeichen*. On 25 October 1943 Hochgarz was added to the Roll of Honour of the German Army for his actions around Welish Witebsk. His company destroyed a further seven T-34s during these actions. On 1 October 1943 Hochgarz was promoted to Hauptmann and Battalion Commander, his unit seeing fierce action in the constant see-sawing actions and counter-attacks between Newel and Witebsk.

On 5 December 1943 Hochgarz was presented with two further *Panzervernichtungsabzeichen* for destroying two more T-34 tanks. By the middle of that month the division was encircled by powerful enemy forces around Newel. Three powerful rings of enemy forces lay between the division and safety. Leading the battalion, Hochgarz successfully broke through the first ring of the encirclement. In the heavy fighting which ensued as the division pushed through the second ring, the regimental commander was killed. Just before noon on that day, Hochgarz was wounded in action yet again, a shell splinter hitting him in the lower abdomen, and in the afternoon as the division successfully forced its way through the final ring of Russian troops, he was once again wounded, this time by a piece of shrapnel from an exploding anti-tank shell. Hochgarz fought on, however, and his gallantry in action leading his men through the heavy Soviet concentrations provided them with an inspiring example to follow. This experienced combat infantryman, tank-hunter and leader of men had proven himself in combat many times. As an ex-ranker himself, he had an excellent rapport with his men who rewarded him with their total loyalty. Several times wounded he had always elected to stay with his men whenever possible. During the final stage of the breakout, however, he was again wounded, this time in the chest by shell shrapnel. With three serious wounds received during this breakout he had no option but to accept evacuation for hospital treatment. On 10 January 1944 Hochgarz was decorated with the Close Combat Clasp in Silver, after taking part in at least 30 individual days of hand-to-hand fighting.

On 15 April 1944 Hochgarz was decorated with the Knight's Cross of the Iron Cross for his gallantry during the breakout in December 1943, and on 1 May he was promoted to Major. Fully recuperated, Major Hochgarz returned to the front on 28 July 1944 at Dünaburg and returned to his old battalion. Just two weeks later he was wounded in action for the eighth time, by grenade splinters, but was able to remain with his men. On 6 September he found himself in command of the entire regiment during an attack on Dorpat. Leading his men from the front as ever, this brave officer was wounded yet again, shrapnel hitting him in the abdomen and sacrum.

Evacuated by hospital ship from Reval in the Kurland pocket to Kiel, Hochgarz was taken to hospital in Dresden where he spent the remainder of the war.

Major Ferdinand Foltin

An Austrian, Ferdinand Foltin was born in Vienna on 30 November 1916. His military career began in September 1936 when he joined Infanterie Regiment 15 of the Austrian Army as a one-year volunteer. A year later, he commenced a course of instruction at the Wiener-Neustadt military academy in order to train for his eventual commissioning as an officer. In May of 1938, while still undergoing training at Wiener-Neustadt after the *Anschluss* with Germany, Foltin was officially drafted into the German army. Completing his pre-commissioning training in September 1938, he joined 6 Kompanie / Infanterie Regiment 107 as a platoon leader with the status of Oberfähnrich. Four months later he was commissioned Leutnant.

The next major step in Foltin's military career came in October 1940 when he joined Parachute Training Course 6 at the Brunswick Para School. On completing his intensive training as a paratroop officer, he was promoted to Oberleutnant, before joining 5 Kompanie of Fallschirmjäger Regiment 3 as a platoon commander. Of course by this time Göring had taken command of all Germany's paratroop forces and consequently on 25 October 1940, Foltin was formally transferred from the army to the Luftwaffe. The next few months were spent on intensive combat training in preparation for the most glorious episode in the history of the Fallschirmjäger, the assault on Crete.

Foltin's regiment was part of 7 Flieger Division, tasked with the capture of Galatas, Canea and Suda Bay. The regiment suffered heavy casualties. In command of his platoon Oberleutnant Foltin displayed such cool gallantry in the most ferocious fighting, despite being wounded, that he was recommended for the Iron Cross First Class. Regulations demanded that a soldier already possess the Iron Cross Second Class before becoming eligible for the First Class. This was neatly circumvented by the simple expedient of awarding him both grades at the same time and on 1 July 1941 Oberleutnant Foltin had both grades of the Iron Cross pinned to his smock. This was a rare occurrence, only permitted in the most deserving of cases. On 1 August he received the wound badge in Black to acknowledge the wounds he had received in action.

Following the Crete battle, Foltin spent a term of duty as a liaison officer at the Officer Training Course for Paratroopers at the Luftwaffe War School Number 2 at Berlin-Gatow. He remained here for eight months, passing on the benefit of his combat experience to the new officers before, in August 1942, rejoining a combat unit of his old regiment as commander of 7 Kompanie / Fallschirmjäger Regiment 3. Foltin then spent a period of combat service on the central sector of the Eastern Front. By February 1943 the division was in the southern sector of the front as part of Heeresgruppe Don, defending the railway lines between Dniepropetrovsk and Stalino. In March the division, badly battered, was pulled out of the line and transferred to the South of France where it was disbanded. Fallschirmjäger Regiment 3 then became part of the newly formed 1 Fallschirm Division. The next few months were spent in training until, in July, it was sent to Sicily. Foltin served as an orderly officer of the divisional staff of 1 Fallschirm Division during the battle for the Catania Plain and saw intense action against British paratroops at Primasole Bridge.

On the conclusion of the campaign in Sicily, 1 Fallschirm Division was withdrawn into Italy where it fought defensive actions against Montgomery's Eighth Army at Foggia before withdrawing up through Italy. In January 1944 Foltin, by now with the rank of Hauptmann, was appointed commander of II Bataillon of Fallschirmjäger Regiment 3 and in April received formal training for appointment as a general staff officer with the Fallschirm Armee Oberkommando before returning to action just in time for the battle of Cassino.

At the time of the third major assault on Cassino, Hauptmann Foltin was a Kampfgruppe commander, in charge of elements of II Bataillon and 10 Kompanie. The 2nd New Zealand Division was to attack the town in a frontal assault while 4th Indian Division attacked Monastery Hill. The assault was to be preceded by a monumental aerial bombardment. On 15 March at 08.30 hours the first wave of Allied bombers began to unload their deadly cargo. More than 1,000 tons of bombs were dropped, followed by a barrage of more than 200,000 artillery shells. Before the attack began II Bataillon had a strength of some 300 men. By the end only 140 were still alive. 1 Fallschirm Division was but a shadow of its former self. These men, however, were not only superbly fit and dedicated soldiers, but were men who knew themselves to be part of an élite formation with morale second to none, even after this terrible bombardment. The rubble left by the bombardment merely provided the tough paras with excellent defensive positions which they exploited to the full in slowing down the Allied advance. Although 7 Kompanie had been reduced to a handful of survivors, Foltin had retained his 6 Kompanie in reserve, sheltered in a cavern some 5 kilometres behind Cassino.

On the second day of the assault, the Fallschirmjäger managed to knock out ten enemy tanks by artillery and anti-tank shells, while their single remaining assault gun took out two further M4 Sherman tanks. The New Zealanders, however, did capture the railway station and on the third day took Hill 193 north of the town of Cassino. Firing smoke charges, the enemy prepared to launch a massed attack on the town. Foltin spotted the danger and quickly resited his few remaining mortars into the best defensive positions. Always cautious enough to keep some forces in reserve, Foltin had only a few men available at his forward positions, and because of heavy Allied fire he would not be able to bring up his reserve until darkness gave them some degree of cover. In the ferocious fighting which ensued, Foltin and his meagre forces were hard pushed to hold off the overwhelmingly superior enemy forces. Heavy armoured forces approached from Via Casilina attacking the German left flank and blasting the damaged houses which the Fallschirmjäger had turned into strongpoints. These were then stormed by Allied infantry. Only at night did it become possible to bring up the reserve, and elements of the Pioniere Bataillon, II Bataillon of Fallschirmjäger Regiment 1 and the Kradschützen Kompanie from the division duly arrived in order to secure Foltin's positions.

Hauptmann Foltin's persistent personal gallantry under enemy attack over a period of some five days of virtually non-stop fighting had been a shining example to his men of the German paratrooper at his best. He had shown a superb grasp of tactics and was always prepared for instant decisions in moving his meagre forces around the battlefield to meet individual dangers as they arose. His skill as a commander, and his personal bravery and disregard of danger were prime factors in the holding of his positions against overwhelming odds.

By 22 March the Allies had called off their offensive for the time being. It was clear to both sides that the reason for the Allied failure was quite simply that the superhuman efforts of 1 Fallschirm Division had defeated everything that the Allies could throw at them. The division was part of Tenth Army, commanded by General von Vietinghoff-Scheel who had reported to his superior, Generalfeldmarschall Kesselring, that no other troops than 1 Fallschirm Division could possibly have held Cassino. High praise indeed, but then the Fallschirmjäger were accustomed to being asked to perform the impossible – and succeeding.

At the end of March the division was withdrawn from the line for a week's well-earned rest before being thrown back into battle. Fallschirmjäger Regiment 4 took over the Monastery position, Fallschirmjäger Regiment 3 the mountain sector and Fallschirmjäger Regiment 1 was held in reserve. When the fourth battle for Cassino began the Allies launched a massive bombardment of unparalleled intensity. More than 1,600 artillery pieces and 3,000 aircraft attacked the weak German defences. Once again the paras of Fallschirmjäger Regiment 3 found themselves in the thick of the action, in bitter hand-to-hand fighting against the tough Polish II Corps.

On 17 May the division was ordered to withdraw as they were in danger of being cut off. Finally forced by circumstances to relinquish their hold on Cassino, the Germans were, however, undefeated in battle. On 9 June 1944 Hauptmann Foltin was decorated with the Knight's Cross of the Iron Cross in reward for his gallantry during the third battle of Cassino. He was also promoted to the rank of Major. On 1 September 1944 Foltin was appointed as General Staff Officer to 7 Fallschirm Division, and saw action in Holland where the division was involved in the counter-attack against the Allied 'Market-Garden' offensive towards Arnhem. The paras were particularly effective in delaying the relief forces of XXX Corps in their attempt to reach the beleaguered British forces in Arnhem.

The division continued to face the British throughout the retreat through Belgium and into north-west Germany. In February 1945 Foltin spent a month undergoing further training as a general staff officer before returning to the division on 1 March. The division saw action opposing the British crossing of the Rhine before finally surrendering in May 1945. Major Foltin was a prisoner of the British until October 1945.

This, however, was by no means the end of Foltin's distinguished military career. In September 1952 he joined the newly reformed Austrian Gendarmerie and over the next 26 years served variously as, company commander, tactics instructor, brigade chief of staff, commander of the advance group of the first Austrian UN contingent in the Congo, commander of the Army Close Combat School, commander of a panzer-grenadier brigade, and Military and Air Attaché in the Austrian Embassies in Ottowa, Prague and East Berlin. When Ferdinand Foltin finally retired from the military in January 1982 at the age of 65 he was a divisional commander.

Among his numerous military decorations are the Paratrooper Badge, the Kreta cufftitle, the Ground Combat Badge of the Luftwaffe, the Golden Merit Award of the Austrian Federal Republic, the Golden Honour Award of the Austrian Federal Republic, the United States Legion of Merit, the Federal Service Awards, Third, Second and First Class, and the Meritorious Service Medal of the National Peoples Army of East Germany.

Few soldiers have had such a full military career as Ferdinand Foltin, and certainly few have ever earned such a wide variety of decorations.

Major Siegfried Jamrowski

Siegfried Jamrowski was born in Angerapp, East Prussia on 1 November 1917. He completed his obligatory six months' service with the Reichsarbeitsdienst between April and September 1936 and then immediately enlisted into Infanterie Regiment 2 in Ortelsburg, Jamrowski served with I Bataillon of this Regiment, which was part of 2 Infanterie Division.

One year after his enlistment, Jamrowski was promoted to the rank of Oberjäger or senior private and on 1 June 1938 was further promoted, to Gefreiter. During the month of August 1938 he attended a special training course at the Infanterieschule Döberitz, and two months later was promoted to Feldwebel. Having completed his military national service he was released from the army as a reservist and commenced a course of study in forestry. He was, however, recalled to the colours on mobilization in 1939.

His first two months of service were taken up in a course for potential officers at the Infanterieschule Döberitz, before joining 4 Kompanie, Infanterie Regiment 2. Thus he missed taking part in the Polish Campaign. From early February 1940 until the end of May Feldwebel Jamrowski served with the regiment's reserve in Allenstein where he was involved in training new recruits.

On 1 June Jamrowski was transferred from the army to the Luftwaffe and from 15 June to 15 July undertook paratroop training at Wittstock, and was awarded his Fallschirmschützen Abzeichen on 25 September. Jamrowski's old unit, 2 Infanterie Division, underwent conversion to an armoured unit, becoming 12th Panzer Division. On 1 September 1940 Leutnant Jamrowski was appointed as a platoon commander in 8 (Maschinengewehr) Kompanie, Fallschirmjäger Regiment 3.

Following the invasion of the Soviet Union in June 1941, the German armies made astonishing progress in the initial stages, reaching the very outskirts of Leningrad in the north and Mariupol in the south by the Sea of Azov. Eventually halted as their supply lines became grossly overstretched, the worn-out Wehrmacht units dug in for the winter. At Leningrad, the Panzer Korps commanded by Generaloberst Höpner was withdrawn on 17 September and moved south to take part in the assault on Moscow. The Russians took full advantage of the weakening of the German forces and pushed units over the River Newa to form bridgeheads at Petruschino and Wyborgskaya. In answer to these threats, elements of 7 Flieger Division were sent in, including Jamrowski's Fallschirmjäger Regiment 3.

The regiment was committed to battle in numerous independent actions. The tough Fallschirmjäger generally achieved their objectives in each case, but only at the cost of heavy losses. Leutnant Jamrowski received the Iron Cross Second Class on 31 October 1941 for his part in these actions. The regiment continued to serve on the Eastern Front in 1942, Jamrowski becoming the adjutant to the regiment's IV Bataillon in February, and being promoted to Oberleutnant in April. In June, he once again took over as a platoon commander with 6 Kompanie of the Regiment.

In the autumn of 1942 7 Flieger Division was disbanded. Fallschirmjäger Regiment 2 became the nucleus of 2 Fallschirm Division, while Fallschirmjäger Regiments 1 and 3 became the core of 1 Fallschirm Division. The new division remained on the Eastern Front initially, and on 25 December 1942 Oberleutnant Jamrowski was awarded the Iron Cross First Class for his bravery in the face of the enemy and efficient command of his company. In late 1942 Jamrowski also qualified for the Ground Assault Badge of the Luftwaffe.

Elements of the division were assembled in France in March 1943 where 1 Fallschirm Division completed its formation. In July 1943 the division was moved to Sicily and played an important part in the defence of the Island. The Fallschirmjäger fought against the British 1 Parachute Brigade which was attempting to capture the Simeto Bridge. The British were repulsed but a later penetration of the German lines near Carlentini led to the encirclement of Fallschirmjäger Regiment 3. In daredevil fashion the Fallschirmjäger escaped the encirclement by crossing *under* the Malati bridge as British tanks rolled over it. The regiment served as cover to the flanks of the main German withdrawal to Messina and was evacuated to the Italian mainland on 17 August.

Fallschirmjäger Regiment 3 saw further fierce action against the Allied landings at Salerno and fought a delaying action as it withdrew up the mainland. The Germans decided to halt the Allied advance at the well-prepared Gustav Line which ran from the east coast near Ortona past Cassino to the west coast between Naples and Anzio. When it became clear to the Allies what the Germans intended they decided to circumvent the German plan by making amphibious landings behind the Gustav Line at Anzio coupled with a massive frontal assault on the Line. The German positions at Cassino dominated the main route to Rome and the Allies were determined to capture these strategic positions. The Germans, however, were equally determined to hold the Allies at bay. Between early January and mid-May a considerable number of assaults by US, French and British forces were rebuffed. The II Bataillon of Fallschirmjäger Regiment 3 moved into positions in Cassino to relieve Grenadier Regiment 211 on 20 February.

When the second battle for Cassino began on 15 March, Jamrowski's paratroopers were subjected to a massive bombardment by the US Air Force. The town was reduced to rubble, which was then mercilessly pounded by artillery fire. The aerial bombardment alone lasted for more than four hours. Each time there was a pause and the Germans thought the attack had ended, a fresh wave of bombers would fly over. Jamrowski reflected that he now knew how U-boat crews felt when suffering a concentrated depth-charge attack. Huddled in the cellars of Cassino, the paras could only wait and pray as the town above them was levelled. One large bomb struck the house in the cellar of which Jamrowski and some of his men were sheltering. As the front of the building began to collapse, the Fallschirmjäger retreated to the cover of the rear of the cellar. The paras were temporarily safe, but rubble and debris had blocked the exit. Each time they attempted to clear a passage, fresh falls of debris blocked the exit again. For twelve hours Jamrowski and his men were trapped until runners from battalion headquarters heard their calls for help and cleared rubble from the outside of the cellar entrance, allowing them to escape. The town of Cassino was unrecognizable, indeed it had all but disappeared. More than seven hundred Allied aircraft had taken part in the bombardment, dropping 1,250 tons of bombs. Unfortunately for the Allies, the accuracy of the bombing had been poor and the aircraft had bombed several of their own positions, causing more than three hundred casualties. If the Allies thought that the Fallschirmjäger had been eliminated by the ferocious bombardment, they were sadly mistaken. Although the Germans had taken a terrible punishment, the rubble created by the bombing made excellent defensive positions, and the attack launched by New Zealand and Indian infantry was beaten back. Despite having lost almost half its strength, the battalion had not lost its indomitable fighting spirit as paratroopers crawled from the rubble and took up their firing positions. In the pause after the first assault, 6 Kompanie under Oberleutnant Jamrowski was transferred to a cavern at the foot of Monastery Hill as battalion reserve. The battalion thus had a fresh company, free of casualties, ready to repulse the next attack. When the New Zealanders launched their next attack, Oberleutnant Jamrowski and the men of 6 Kompanie were ready for them. Jamrowski not only conducted a spirited defence of his positions, repulsing every attack launched against him, but actually succeeded in a number of counter-attacks, dealing a severe blow against the New Zealanders.

Ferocious in both defence and attack, the Fallschirmjäger at Cassino also had a great respect for the gallantry and fighting spirit of the Allied troops pitted against them. On Hill 435, a number of Gurkhas had been cut off after fierce fighting in which they suffered dreadful losses. When the second battle of Cassino was called off the plucky Gurkhas were stranded. They solved the problem themselves by raising a Red Cross flag, and walked away from their positions carrying their wounded, right under the eyes of the paratroopers. Although many of the Gurkhas were unharmed and capable of fighting, the Germans magnanimously allowed their gallant enemy to withdraw unmolested.

The respect, in turn, in which the Germans were held by the Allies can be gauged by General Alexander's comment that 1 Fallschirm Division was 'the best German Division on *any* front'.

Even such superhuman efforts could not prevent the inevitable, and sheer weight of numbers eventually allowed the Allies to turn the German flanks. It was decided to withdraw the Fallschirmjäger from Cassino rather than lose them to an Allied encirclement. They had already done far more than could have been expected of them and now the paratroops withdrew, defeated by circumstances, but not beaten in battle. They would go with their heads held high and their *espirit de corps* and fighting reputation as a truly élite force greatly enhanced.

On 9 June 1944, Siegfried Jamrowski, 'Jambo' to his men, was decorated with the Knight's Cross of the Iron Cross for his repeated heroism in the fiercest of fighting. His fearlessness was an inspiration to his men, spurring them on to ever greater efforts despite the overwhelming superiority of the enemy.

Fallschirmjäger Regiment 3 went on to defend the approaches to Rome before moving to the Adriatic front where it went into battle at Bologna before withdrawing farther up the Italian mainland. It finally surrendered to the British on 2 May 1945, Jamrowski by then having achieved the rank of Major. He was held in British captivity until 24 April 1946 when he was released.

SS-Unterscharführer Emil Dürr

During the historic Normandy battles in the summer of 1944, countless acts of gallantry were performed on both sides. Reputations of both units and commanders were made and destroyed. Few units gained such a reputation for fanatical determination and reckless gallantry than the youths of the 12th SS Panzer Division Hitlerjugend.

Formed at the beginning of 1943, this Division was made up of boys of the Hitler Youth stiffened by a cadre of experienced officers and NCOs from the élite Leibstandarte SS Adolf Hitler as well as other Waffen-SS and army units. The average age in the unit was just 17 years. Only some 3 per cent of the divisional strength was over 25. Its commanders were formidable soldiers, mostly highly decorated Leibstandarte veterans such as SS-Brigadeführer Fritz Witt, SS-Oberführer Kurt 'Panzer' Meyer, SS-Obersturmbannführer Max Wünsche, SS-Obersturmbannführer Gerd Bremer and SS-Sturmbannführer Hein

Springer, all *Ritterkreutzträger*, with years of combat experience in Germany's premier élite unit.

With a high level of equipment, something that few German units could boast at this stage of the war, and the fanatical loyalty of its politically indoctrinated young soldiers, the division looked like a formidable proposition on paper, but how would it perform? The division gave a good account of itself in training near Beverloo in Belgium and its commanders were confident it would acquit itself well, which indeed it most certainly did. The division moved into France in the last few hours before the Allied landings, to be based just south of Rouen. On the morning of 6 June it was ordered to Lisieux to counter-attack Canadian forces in that area. Almost immediately the divisional vehicles came under attack from Allied rocket-firing fighters before reaching the area around the Ardenne Abbey where it went into cover. As the Canadians headed for the Carpiquet airfield, the tanks of Max Wünsche's SS Panzer Regiment 12 struck and the over-confident Canadians were thrown back in disarray with severe losses in both men and tanks. The Hitlerjugend Division had survived its first major combat engagement, but though it had acquitted itself well, its losses could not be made up as quickly and easily as could those of the Allies.

At dawn on the morning of 26 June 1944, the Allies began a ferocious bombardment of the divisional positions. For a full three hours, artillery salvoes crashed down on the front-line area around St Mauvieu and the town itself. Men and equipment were mercilessly ripped asunder, munition trucks and dumps were hit and erupted in a fury of flame and destruction and houses were reduced to rubble. Telegraph poles were reduced to matchwood and the air was filled with deadly shrapnel. Shortly after the barrage ended, Dürr's battalion HQ came under attack from a force of some fifteen M4 Sherman tanks. The HQ was the last bastion of defence, preventing an Allied breakthrough towards Caen–Falaise. The small force defending the HQ were equipped with light automatic weapons only. As if the situation were not desperate enough, a flame-thrower tank appeared.

SS-Unterscharführer Emil Dürr immediately volunteered to tackle the tank. Picking up a Panzerfaust he vaulted over the wall, took aim and fired but his shot missed its target. Now the enemy tanks turned on him and opened fire with their machine-guns. Dürr was hit in the chest but managed to make his way back to cover. Furious at his failure, he snatched up a second Panzerfaust and set off again despite his wound and his comrade's attempts to dissuade him. Alerted to his presence now, the Allied tanks once again drove him back with machine-gun fire. Dürr knew that if the flame-thrower were not knocked out they were finished so, despite the enemy machine-gun fire ran forward, zigzagging towards the target, this time carrying a satchel charge.

Miraculously reaching the tank unscathed, he placed the charge on its hull and waited for the explosion. The charge fell off. Dürr ran forward, picked it up and held it to the tank's hull, knowing full well that his own life would probably be forfeit.

The charge exploded and the tank burst into flames. Dürr felt a tremendous punch in his chest as the blast flung him away like a rag doll, to lie paralysed by the excruciating pain of his mutilated limbs. In despair, despite his chest wound and mutilated legs, he managed to drag himself back to his men who pulled him into cover and summoned a medical orderly. Nothing could be done for him other than to make him as comfortable as possible as his life ebbed away. His comrades carried him to the shade of a tree in a small hollow and gently laid him down. He asked to be propped up so that he could see what was happening, but smoke and flames obscured the scene 'Is it gone?' he asked. His comrades gently removed his helmet and laid him back down, his gas mask container used as a pillow. Dürr asked for a cigarette. His grief stricken comrades knew the end was near. He lay, quiet and thoughtful, his blue eyes clear, then turned to his comrades and said, 'Say hello to my wife, and the little ones – and look after yourselves.' Dürr then closed his eyes, took one last deep breath, and was still.

The 24-year-old NCO from Mühlacher in Wurttemberg had already shown sufficient courage in action to win both the Second and First Class Iron Crosses in June, and when word of his self-sacrifice reached division, he was immediately recommended for the Knight's Cross of the Iron Cross. When it was approved on 23 August, Dürr became the first junior NCO of the division to recieve the award.

Oberleutnant Erich Lepkowski

Erich Lepkowski was born in Giesen, East Prussia on 17 September 1919. His career as a soldier began on 1 June 1938 with his national service as a member of Infanterie Regiment 1 in Königsberg. On 1 September 1939 he transferred from the Army to the Luftwaffe Signals branch where he trained as a flight crew radio operator. In August 1940, still serving as a radio operator, Lepkowski was posted to the regimental signals troop of Fallschirmjäger Regiment 2 in Berlin.

During the Balkans Campaign of 1940, the regiment was tasked to block the sole escape route for the Allied troops retreating towards the Peloponnese by capturing the bridge crossing the Corinth Canal. The Fallschirmjäger landed by glider, under heavy fire from the defenders of the bridge. Although the bridge was seized, the Allies launched a furious counter-attack, putting the Germans under great pressure until the arrival of reinforcements secured the position. All looked well and the demolition charges set by the Allies were removed and stacked at the side of the bridge. The stack was hit by a stray shell from a British gun and in the resultant explosion the bridge was destroyed and several German pioneers were killed. Lepkowski served as NCO in command of the signals section of 4 Kompanie during the Corinth battle.

On the successful conclusion of the Balkan campaign, Fallschirm-jäger Regiment 2 was tasked to capture the airfield and town of Retimo during the historic battle for Crete. In fierce fighting against tough Australian infantry, some 7,000 strong, the regiment was under heavy pressure until the arrival of a regiment of General Ringel's Gebirgsjäger strengthened the German force sufficiently to drive off the Australians, and capture more than 1,000 prisoners.

With the end of the successful but costly Crete operation, and Hitler's decision to prohibit further large-scale paratroop operations, the regiment was transferred to the Eastern Front where it served in the southern sector near Taganrog and the Rivier Mius. Utilized in straightforward infantry operations, these élite, hard-bitten paras fought superbly, but, as with most élite units, their determination and fearless gallantry cost them many casualties. In this first year in Russia, more than 3,000 veteran paras were killed. Even at this early stage in the war, Germany could ill afford to lose men of such calibre. Fallschirmjäger Regiment 2 was subsequently transferred to the far north of the Front, to the area around the Wolchow where it distinguished itself during the defensive battles after the Soviet push to try to break the siege of Leningrad.

In the spring the Fallschirmjäger were withdrawn from the Eastern Front and sent to France for rest and refitting. On 1 April 1942 Lepkowski was promoted to Oberfeldwebel.

Returning to the Front in the late autumn of 1942, the regiment was located north of Smolensk and saw much furious fighting around Orel and Velikje Luki. On 20 April 1943 Lepkowski was commissioned Leutnant and went on to become a platoon commander in 5 Kompanie of Fallschirmjäger Regiment 2. The regiment had been withdrawn from the Front to become the nucleus of the newly constituted 2 Fallschirm Division along with Fallschirmjäger Regiments 6 and 7, under the command of Generalmajor Ramcke. It then moved briefly to Italy where its formation was completed. It took part in the disarming of Italian units after the Italian capitulation in September and was used to gain control of Rome. Late in the year it was transported back to the Leningrad Front, leaving behind part of its strength to be used as a cadre for yet another newly formed unit, Fallschirm Division. Back on the Eastern Front, Lepkowski and his platoon were pushed to the limit in hard combat. In the space of just 30 days, his platoon carried out 48 fighting reconnaissance missions.

On the night of 18/19 December II Bataillon / Fallschirmjäger Regiment 2 was involved in an attack on the heights around Perwomaisk but encountered strong Russian infantry forces with armoured support which pushed them back and seemed likely to break through the German lines. Lepkowski realized the danger and gathering together all the paras he could muster and supported by three self-propelled assault guns, he launched an immediate attack. The ferocity of the German counter-attack halted the Russians, and prevented a dangerous breakthrough. On 20 December Lepkowski was appointed battalion adjutant. On the following day, the commander of 5 Kompanie, Oberleutnant Nowarra, was killed in action on Hill 167 at Nowgorodka. Lepkowski was appointed to take his place.

On 21 December Leutnant Lepkowski led his company into the attack on the hill against heavy defensive fire from the Russians, some two battalions strong. After two hours of fierce hand-to-hand fighting, Lepkowski's men finally wrested control of the hill from the enemy. For this achievement, Leutnant Lepkowski was decorated with the German Cross in Gold on 25 December 1943. The Russians launched sixteen attempts to retake the hill. In bitter combat the gallant paras doggedly defended their positions, but were eventually reduced to a strength of just seventeen men. Lepkowski held out for a full seven days before being forced to withdraw, under cover of darkness. Although the Russians re-took the hill, their attempted breakthrough had been greatly delayed thanks to the gallantry of Erich Lepkowski. Not for the first time had a tiny force of determined Fallschirmjäger held off greatly superior forces, proving yet again that their élite status was richly deserved. The regimental commander, Oberstleutnant Koch, recommended Lepkowski for the Knight's Cross of the Iron Cross. It was in fact the second time that he had been recommended for this award.

The division was once again withdrawn from the Eastern Front in April and was refitted in Germany before being allocated to the French port of Brest. By August of 1944, the US VIII Corps under General Middleton were determinedly laying siege to the beleaguered garrison. Once again, Lepkowski was to display courage of the highest order. Having been informed of a group of Fallschirmjäger cut off behind enemy lines, he commandeered a motley collection of naval vehicles, together with an armoured car and a mobile anti-aircraft gun, broke through the surrounding US positions, travelled some 60 kilometres through enemy-held territory and rescued some 113 paras from II Bataillon, Fallschirmjäger Regiment 2, taking, along the way, some 62 French partisans prisoner. He then fought his way back through the American lines into the relative safety of the Brest garrison. On 21 August 1944, Oberleutnant Lepkowski was awarded the Knight's

Cross of the Iron Cross for his conspicuous gallantry. The award had been officially approved on 8 August. The Brest garrison held out against vastly superior enemy forces until 20 September 1944 when it finally surrendered to the Americans. Lepkowski was held as a prisoner of war until July 1947.

On 1 April 1960 Erich Lepkowski returned to military service when he joined the Federal German Army, the Bundesheer. In 1962 he was promoted to Hauptmann, serving in the Luftlande Division. He made more than 600 parachute jumps with the Bundesheer. Promoted to Major in October 1970, he ultimately reached the rank of Oberstleutnant in 1973 before retiring in 1974.

Erich Lepkowski, a gallant soldier in the finest traditions of the élite Fallschirmjäger, died in Saarbrücken in May 1975.

Obergefreiter Franz Weber

Franz Weber was born on 30 November 1921, the son of farmer Adam Weber and his wife Anna, in Futog, in the Novi Sad district of Yugoslavia. From 1927 to 1933 he attended Volksschule and from 1935 to 1938, learned the trade of baker. Completing his vocational training, he obtained his journeyman's papers as a baker and moved to Germany in 1941, becoming an assistant to master baker Richard Rullenberg in Stettin. He was eventually called up for military service in September 1942 at the age of 21. On completion of his basic induction training he joined 1/ Infanterie Ersatz Bataillon 374 in Idriza, Russia. In December 1942 he was posted to his first combat unit, 8 Kompanie / Jäger Regiment 28 in Staraja Russa in the Demjansk pocket. Weber was promoted to Gefreiter on 1 April 1943.

In the autumn of 1944 Weber was still serving with 8 Kompanie of Jäger Regiment 28 when the unit was tasked to capture Hill 1387 in the Rodna Pass. The grassy, overgrown pyramid-shaped hill was defended by an extensive trench system covered by machine-gun positions originally built by the Hungarian Army. The hill was strategically very important, with a fine field of fire over the roads nearby which were used as a main supply route. Unfortunately for the Germans the enemy had captured the hill and now menaced the German supply columns. The hill had to be recaptured quickly and the task fell to Weber and his comrades.

Weber's company had already been reduced by previous actions to just forty men, but the Germans doggedly advanced over the ground, which offered little cover from enemy fire. Soon mortar and machine-gun fire forced the advancing Germans to halt and take whatever cover they could find.

Weber and his section, led by a young officer cadet, was on the left flank of the company. Creeping forward with his comrades, Weber found an abandoned machine-gun position, long unused and apparently of First World War vintage. The enemy were only some 40 metres distant, with a hollow between the opposing positions. Weber's team set up their machine-gun and provided covering fire while Weber crawled into the hollow. Having got as close as possible, Weber started to throw hand-grenades, but the Russians opened fire with their machine-gun and attempted to throw back his grenades before they exploded. A couple of successful hits soon cleared them out, however, and Weber's comrade on the machine-gun rushed over to occupy the abandoned enemy position while Weber returned to his company commander to report the capture of one of the enemy's key machine-gun positions. He found the company was still pinned down by machine-gun fire, and unable to advance over the open terrain. Weber immediately offered to attempt to take out the enemy position, and set off with a fresh supply of hand-grenades. Despite being wounded as he cautiously edged his way towards the enemy, Weber pushed on and eventually reached a position near enough to throw his grenades. They landed on target and the machine-gun was silenced. Weber's unit immediately recommended him for the Knight's Cross. The award was approved on 28 October 1944. Weber meanwhile was evacuated to hospital in Liegniz. While recovering, at a ceremony in the hospital, the Knight's Cross was draped around his neck on 30 November 1944.

Weber took part in several more fierce defensive actions against the Red Army, winning the Close Combat Clasp for hand-to-hand fighting on 26 December 1944. Forced back into East Prussia, his division was finally captured by the Russians in May 1945. Whilst being marched into captivity, Weber was able to escape during a rest break. There were so many German soldiers in the long column of weary prisoners that he was not missed. He managed to make his way into Austria and eventually reached Vienna where he hoped to be able to arrange transport back to his home in Yugoslavia, but he was recaptured by the Russians and held in the barracks at Wiener–Albrecht for one month before being moved to Mödling on the way to a prisoner-of-war camp at Sopron in Hungary from where, in September 1945, he was released. Again Weber tried to return to Yugoslavia, but was prevented from doing so by partisans who, virtually a law unto themselves, were active along the Hungarian and Yugoslav border. Once more Weber returned to Austria where he managed to find work in the Soviet-controlled zone. Eventually he managed to slip over the border into the US zone and made his way to Bavaria where he was fortunate enough to locate his family in Müncheberg. They had been driven out of their homes, as had so many thousands of ethnic

Germans in Yugoslavia, by Slavs seeking revenge against the German community. Looking for work, Weber and his family moved to Munich where, after a short spell working for a builder's firm, he returned to his trade as a baker. Franz Weber married in 1949 and has two children. Eventually, Weber had to give up baking for health reasons and took work with the giant Siemens firm where he worked as a turner for twenty-five years, until 1981. Weber now lives in well-earned retirement.

Major Heinz Meyer

Heinz Meyer was born in Magdeburg on 9 April 1916. At the age of 21 he enlisted in 14 (Fallschirm) Kompanie of the élite Regiment General Göring. On 1 April 1938 Meyer left General Goring when the Fallschirm Kompanie was transferred to become the cadre of the newly formed Fallschirmjäger Regiment 1. Gefreiter Meyer served in 4 Kompanie of this new regiment. In January 1939 Meyer was attached to the regimental staff for one month before attending a two-month course for NCOs. In October he was promoted to Obergefreiter and in November to Unteroffizier.

Clearly Meyer had shown considerable promise and had been selected for rapid promotion. In April 1940 he was nominated as an officer candidate, attending an officer's training course at Berlin-Gatow. On 1 May 1940 Meyer was promoted to Feldwebel, just a few days before making his first combat jump during the invasion of Holland. Meyer served with II Bataillon, Fallschirmjäger Regiment 1, tasked with capturing the Moerdyk and Dordrecht bridges. Meyer saw action at the successful capture of the Moerdyk bridge which the paras held for three days until relief arrived in the form of 9th Panzer Division. Feldwebel Meyer was awarded the Iron Cross Second Class for his part in the action.

After the successful conclusion of the Western Campaign, Meyer was commissioned Leutnant on 1 August 1940 and appointed as a platoon commander in 11 Kompanie, Fallschirmjäger Regiment 3. With his new regiment Leutnant Meyer saw action in Greece where, temporarily attached to Fallschirmjäger Regiment 2, he took part in the capture of the Corinth Canal. During the battle for Crete Meyer saw action at Galatas, Canea and Suda Bay, winning the Iron Cross First Class for these actions, although the award was not made until 21 June.

After the successful conclusion of the battle for Crete, the Fallschirmjäger moved to the Russian Front, serving on the northern sector near Leningrad. On 20 February 1942 he was transferred to III Bataillon, Fallschirmjäger Regiment 4, still serving on the Leningrad front. In July he was promoted to Oberleutnant. In the autumn of 1942 a new para unit, 1 Fallschirm Division, was formed. The bulk of the division's strength came from the former 7 Flieger Division, and included Fallschirmjäger Regiment 4. Initially, the new unit remained on the Russian Front, but in March 1943 it was withdrawn and sent to France to complete its working-up and engage in further intensive training. In July it was committed to action in the defence of Sicily and saw bitter fighting at Primasole Ridge against British paras. Just before Sicily fell, the division was withdrawn to the Italian mainland. Here again the Fallschirmjäger were involved in bitter defensive battles, facing troops of Montgomery's Eighth Army at Foggia. Throughout the winter of 1943/44 the Germans were slowly pushed up the 'leg' of the Italian mainland.

In February 1 Fallschirm Division moved into positions at Cassino to relieve 90th Panzer Grenadier Division. Here the Fallschirmjäger were to win undying glory in their steadfast defence against overwhelming odds. On 21 February II Bataillon, Fallschirmjäger Regiment 4 moved into position on Calvary Hill, to the north-west of the Monastery. On 19 March a New Zealand armoured force attacked Massa Albaneta, hoping to link up with Gurkha and Indian troops there. Although taken by surprise, Meyer and his men sprang into action against the enemy tanks, using bazookas and Teller mines. Six tanks were destroyed and a further sixteen disabled. By halting this armoured attack Meyer and his men had removed a dangerous threat to the Monastery. Attacking tanks with hand-held weapons such as Teller mines takes nerves of steel and for his gallantry during the annihilation of the enemy armoured attack, Meyer was decorated with the Knight's Cross of the Iron Cross on 8 April 1944.

On 17 May 1944 Meyer was given command of III Bataillon of the newly formed Fallschirmjäger Regiment 15. This was part of 5 Fallschirm Division which had taken over III Bataillon of Fallschirmjäger Regiment 4. Following the Allied landings in Normandy in June 1944, 5 Fallschirm Division was part of General Meindl's II Fallschirm Korps facing American troops near St-Lô. Despite continual attacks by Allied aircraft, the Fallschirmjäger gave a good account of themselves against the US 2nd Infantry Division. Fighting alongside 17 SS Panzer Grenadier Division Götz von Berlichingen, the Fallschirmjäger put up a most determined resistance to the Allied advance, but the sheer overwhelming *matériel* superiority of the enemy eventually allowed them to break out from St-Lô. By August the Fallschirmjäger were themselves very nearly cut off in the Falaise pocket and barely escaped capture. Meyer subsequently served at Arnhem and in the Ardennes offensive. He was awarded the Oakleaves to his Knight's Cross on 18 November 1944 for his continued gallantry in action and inspiring leadership in the Normandy battles and in Holland.

By March 1945 Hauptmann Meyer was commanding a Kampf-gruppe fighting against the Americans in the Harz mountains. He was taken prisoner by the Americans on 8 May 1945, ending his war with the rank of Major and as one of the highest decorated officers of the Fallschirmjager.

Obergefreiter Eduard Hug

Born on 23 September 1921, Eduard Hug commenced his military career in February 1941, having previously spent four months training with the Reichsarbeitsdienst. He joined 1 Kompanie, Jäger Regiment 75, part of 5 Infanterie Division as a private while it was preparing for the invasion of the Soviet Union.

The division took part in extremely heavy fighting around the Vyasma area, suffering considerable losses. During this period Hug qualified as a combat infantryman, earning the Infantry Assault Badge. In December the division was considered to have been so badly battered that it was withdrawn from combat and sent to France for rest and refitting. During the refit it was reclassified as a Jäger division and returned to the Eastern Front in February 1942, allocated to Heeres-gruppe Nord. During March and April Hug served with the regiment in the relief of the German units encircled in the Demjansk pocket. He earned the East Front Campaign Medal in July and was promoted to the rank of Obergefreiter.

During the winter of 1942/3 as part of Sixteenth Army, Hug and his regiment fought in the ferocious battles around Staraya Russa before moving to the northern sector of the front to defend the approaches to the Polish border. During the retreat north-west from the Bug, Obergefreiter Hug had so distinguished himself for gallantry as to be awarded the Iron Cross Second Class and First Class within just two days, the Second Class on 2 August and the First Class on 4 August.

On 2 September the division was once again involved in desperate defensive actions against the inexorable Russian advance. Oberge-freiter Hug lay in his foxhole with his MG-42 machine-gun awaiting an enemy attack and his position soon came under a furious assault. Having no clear field of fire himself, Hug was horrified when the machine-gun covering the area fell silent, its crew killed by enemy fire. Hug realized the danger and taking up his own machine-gun leapt from his position and ran towards the knocked out machine-gun position. As he ran, he saw some seventy or so enemy troops approaching fast and realized that he would never make it. He stopped where he was, totally exposed to enemy fire, and slung his MG-42 by its strap from his shoulder and opened fire. The machine-gun, with its exceptionally high rate of fire, tore into the enemy ranks and they quickly retreated. Hug quickly got himself into the foxhole and set up his machine-gun. Six further attempts were made by the Russians to storm Hug's position, but each time his accurate fire drove them back.

As the light began to fade, a seventh attack was launched. The enemy assault troops ran forward firing their machine pistols and covered by heavy fire from their own machine-gun positions. Each time Hug attempted to return fire he was forced to duck to avoid the intense machine-gun fire. Unable to attain his previous deadly accuracy, Hug did the best he could, but the enemy gradually drew closer and were soon within 30 metres of his position. Hand-grenades began to fall around his foxhole. To Hug's horror, his machine-gun had a stoppage and he hadn't time to clear it. Hug did not panic, however, and quickly began to throw his hand-grenades. The leading enemy troops faltered slightly and the precious moments gave him time to clear the gun. Hug now opened fire once again and his machine-gun scythed great gaps in the enemy ranks. The survivors panicked and ran, leaving some sixty dead around Hug's isolated position. During the night troops from the regimental reserve came forward and closed the gaps in the German front. The position was secured.

Acting entirely on his own initiative, and with total disregard for his own safety, Hug had succeeded in single-handedly preventing an enemy breakthrough. His grateful divisional commander recommended him for the Knight's Cross of the Iron Cross for his great gallantry and this was awarded on 2 September 1944. The young corporal had won the Iron Crosses Second and First Class and the Knight's Cross all within just over one month.

Hug's division continued its fighting withdrawal through Poland and into the eastern provinces of Germany. Drawn into the defence of Berlin, it was decimated there and Hug and the rest of the division's survivors were taken into captivity. He survived the ordeal and now lives in retirement.

Oberleutnant Wolfgang von Bostell

Born on 25 January 1917 in Heiningen, Wolfgang Hans Heiner Paul von Bostell joined the Wehrmacht in October 1935 when he enlisted in 2 Batterie, Artillerie Regiment 48. After one year's artillery experience Gefreiter von Bostell transferred to the anti-tank arm of the artillery, joining Panzer Abwehr Abteilung 12. Promoted Obergefreiter in October 1937 and Unteroffizier in March 1938, von Bostell was a section leader in 2 Kompanie, Panzer Jäger Abteilung 12. This was part of 12 Infanterie Division, a Mecklenburg unit which was based in Pomerania. Unteroffizier von Bostell saw service with the division in

Poland and during the attack on France where his proficiency in charge of his gun team won him the Iron Cross Second Class on 11 June 1940. On 17 November he was promoted Feldwebel.

In the summer of 1941, von Bostell and his unit took part in the invasion of the Soviet Union as part of 16 Armee fighting on the northern sector of the front. The division served with distinction, von Bostell himself winning the Iron Cross First Class on 4 July. On 22 July he was seriously wounded. Evacuated for treatment, on his release he joined the 'Convalescent Company' of Panzer Jäger Ersatz Abteilung 2. On his full recovery, von Bostell returned to the Front, as a section leader in 2 Kompanie, Panzer Jäger Abteilung 12 and saw action at the relief of the Demjansk pocket where 12 Infanterie Division was a major part of the relief force which broke through to the encircled troops of II Corps. During this action, von Bostell was once again seriously wounded.

In October 1942 Feldwebel von Bostell became a section leader in 1 Kompanie of Panzer Jäger Abteilung 23, fighting on the Volchow Front as part of 23 Infanterie Division. This was a newly formed division which took over the divisional number of the original 23 Infanterie Division which had been reformed as 26th Panzer Division. On 16 April 1943 Feldwebel von Bostell was nominated as an officer candidate with the status of Fahnenjunker-Feldwebel, and from 6 August until 23 November of that year attended an officer's training course at Wischau. By the end of this course he was a senior officer cadet with the rank of Oberfähnrich. Almost immediately he attended another, lasting until March 1944, for senior officer cadets of the Panzertruppe, near Berlin. Shortly after completing this course he was commissioned Leutnant. Leutnant von Bostell then attended the Sturmgeschütz School at Mielau in Poland before, in April 1944, rejoining 23 Infanterie Division as a platoon commander with 2 Kompanie, Panzer Jäger (Sturmgeschütz) Abteilung 1023. The Sturm-geschütz was a self-propelled gun mounted on the chasis of the Panzer Mk III. Initially intended as an infantry support weapon, it became an essential part of the equipment of most major German units. Cheaper to build than a tank, it was almost as effective, its low superstructure making it a difficult target. Its only real drawback was its lack of a turret, and thus very limited traverse of the main armament. These weapons became very effective tank killers and were used by many Panzer-Jäger units as well as in their original role as assault artillery.

The unit remained on the northern sector of the Front where it fought in a defensive role against the Russian breakout after the siege of Leningrad was broken. Subsequently the division withdrew into Estonia defending Saareman Island against a large Russian invasion force.

In the summer of 1944 Leutnant von Bostell received the Demjansk Shield for his part in that epic battle the previous year. By August of 1944 his Abteilung was located around Modohn in Latvia. On 11 August Leutnant von Bostell's Sturmgeschützen were advancing in support of an attack by the division's grenadiers. Shortly before reaching the battle area, the attack team met the divisional commander, rifle in hand, with a number of Russian prisoners. Generalmajor Wisselinck had personally led his grenadiers into the attack and now sought the assistance of von Bostell in tackling the enemy tanks. One of the footsoldiers hitched a ride forward on von Bostell's Sturmgeschütz and, using tracer ammunition, marked the known positions of the enemy T-34s. In minutes six tanks were knocked out and the Russians began to panic. A number of other T-34s immediately retreated leaving the Russian infantry without their armoured support.

In the early hours of the following morning, however, the Russians renewed their attack. The Sturmgeschützen rolled forward and, cresting a small hillock, found themselves in the midst of an enemy position. The camouflaged Russian troops, ready to attack the German positions, thought the Sturmgeschützen were their own tanks and waved them forward. Von Bostell calmly waved back to the Russian infantrymen and slowly moved towards the German dugouts. Suddenly two T-34s went charging past the slowly moving assault guns. Keeping his cool, von Bostell waited until the enemy tanks were about 60 feet in front of him and opened fire. Both T-34s burst into flames. All hell then let loose. From all hatches and vision ports the crews of the Sturmgeschützen poured machine-gun and machine pistol fire on the enemy. Two more T-34s slowly emerged from a small copse. These were quickly dispatched by the high-velocity 75mm guns of the Sturmgeschützen. In the midst of the furious fighting one of von Bostell's tracks broke a link. The Sturmgeschütz could now only turn in circles. At that moment von Bostell spied the turret of an enemy tank, its hull partly concealed by a small hillock. Slowly the Sturmgeschütz revolved on the spot, bringing its gun to bear and the enemy tank was soon added to von Bostell's score. Then the motor broke down and refused to re-start.

Disabled as it was, the Sturmgeschütz would be easy prey to the enemy infantry, but at that point the German infantry, seeing the danger in the situation, came storming out of their dugouts and drove off the enemy. In the two-day action, von Bostell had knocked out eleven enemy tanks and prevented a breakthrough by the Russians. This was no long-distance engagement with tanks picking one another off at extreme range, but close combat in the thick of an enemy infantry force which could have disabled their Sturmgeschütz at any time. Despite the extreme danger, von Bostell had not panicked, but had calmly knocked out all the enemy tanks which appeared. Even when his Sturmgeschütz was disabled he did not abandon it but continued to fight. All von Bostell's crew were decorated with the Iron Cross, both Second and First Classes, and von Bostell himself was recommended for the Knight's Cross which was approved and awarded on 2 September.

Having been wounded in action again on 22 August, he was still recovering when his award was announced, and the Knight's Cross was hung around his neck by the senior surgeon at the Quedlinburg hospital on 24 September 1944.

After having fully recovered, Leutnant von Bostell was posted to 2 Kompanie of Panzer Jäger Abteilung 205, part of 205 Infanterie Division in Kurland. This division had already proved itself during the defensive battles of 1944, and with it von Bostell was to enhance his own personal reputation as a fearless daredevil. Operating south of Libau, von Bostell personally led seventeen counter-attacks against the opposing Red Army units in just six days, between 3 and 8 March 1945. His unfailing efforts led to the failure of an attempted Russian breakthrough and he was wounded in action for the tenth time during these operations.

On 26 March 1945, during the Kurland battles, the Russians had forced a small breakthrough in the German lines which they were seeking to exploit. The division was tasked to prevent the enemy expanding the bridgehead they had forced. At this time Panzer Jäger Abteilung 1205 was part of the defending forces. Part of the Abteilung, Jagd Panzer Kompanie 1205, was a component of Kampfgruppe Berg which was thrown into action against the Russians. The company was split into two troops, with three tank killers in each troop. Leutnant von Bostell's troop was tasked to attack the enemy bridgehead from the north while the other troop attacked from the south. The infantry would then attack towards the east and trap the enemy between the two armoured units, forcing them back.

Leutnant von Bostell and his troop made rapid progress to their launch-point for the attack, only to hear over the radio that the other troop had run into an enemy minefield and was unable to progress. Knowing the urgency of the situation, von Bostell split his own force and went straight into the attack. After knocking out several enemy positions and taking some prisoners, his own Sturmgeschütz was hit by a 122mm anti-tank shell and had to withdraw into some wooded cover. His Sturmgeschütz disabled, he nevertheless returned fire on the enemy gun position and destroyed it after a few well-placed shots. Abandoning his disabled vehicles, von Bostell was picked up by one of the other Sturmgeschützen.

Meanwhile the enemy had established another anti-tank gun

position and opened fire on the two remaining Sturmgeschützen. Moving to attack this new danger, von Bostell's Sturmgeschütz ran on to a mine and was disabled. The last remaining Sturmgeschütz, however, scored direct hits on the enemy position, destroying two anti-tank guns and capturing a third. Leutnant von Bostell now transferred to the third Sturmgeschütz and carried on his attack still further, destroying several more enemy positions before the last Sturmgeschütz was also disabled. Subsequently reinforcements arrived from Sturmgeschütz Brigade 9122 and von Bostell was soon in action again. By the end of this action, von Bostell's troop of Sturmgeschützen had destroyed forty machine-gun positions, one heavy infantry howitzer and eight anti-tank guns as well as costing the enemy some 450 dead. His personal score of enemy tanks destroyed at this stage stood at 28.

Leutnant von Bostell was decorated with the Oakleaves to his Knight's Cross on 30 April 1945 for his continued gallantry in action. On 1 May 1945 von Bostell was promoted to Oberleutnant and just one week later went into Russian captivity. He was held prisoner for eight long years, being released in October 1953.

Major Heinrich Keese

Born on 18 April 1918 in Unsen, Heinrich Keese was the son of a train driver of the Deutsche Reichsbahn (railway service). He attended Volksschule in Holtensen and the Realschule in Hameln. On completing his education he trained as an industrial salesman. In April 1938, Keese began his period of compulsory service in the Reichsarbeitsdienst and was involved in the construction of the Siegfried Line. He completed his six months with the RAD, attaining the rank of Obervormann.

At the age of 20, Keese volunteered for military service and on 11 November 1938 joined Pionier Bataillon 20, a motorized combat engineer unit from Hamburg. By the outbreak of war in September 1939, he was serving as a messenger and clerk with the batallion staff and served in this capacity during the Polish Campaign around Brest-Litovsk. This was the first action seen by the battalion, its parent unit, 20 Infanterie Division, only having been raised in 1935–6.

On 28 February 1940 Keese was promoted to Gefreiter and posted to 3 Kompanie of the Bataillon. He served as machine-gunner and second in charge of his section during the attack on France, being wounded for the first time near Arras. He recovered quickly from his wounds, however, and was soon back with his comrades. On 1 November 1940 he was promoted to Obergefreiter and section leader. Five weeks later he received the Deutscher Schutzwall Ehrenzeichen for his part in the construction of the Siegfried Line defences. On 1

December 1940 Keese was promoted to Unteroffizier, having completed a three-month training course with his battalion for NCOs.

At the commencement of Operation 'Barbarossa', the invasion of the Soviet Union, 20 Infanterie Division fought as part of Army Group Centre. By now the division had been regraded from infantry to panzer grenadier and fought well at Smolensk, the crossing of the Dnieper and at Minsk. Keese proved himself a good junior NCO and was decorated with the Iron Cross Second Class on 13 July 1941 for his efficiency and determination in combat. Subsequently sent to the northern sector of the front, fighting at the crossing of the River Dvina and the push to Oreshek near Leningrad, Keese showing sufficient flair during these fierce battles to win the Iron Cross First Class on 6 June 1942. From 20 June to 1 October Keese attended an officer's training course at the Pionierschule at Dessau, being promoted Fahnenjunker Feldwebel on 1 September, and on the successful completion of his course he was commissioned Leutnant.

Leutnant Keese returned to his battalion and served as a platoon commander. He was then posted to a replacement unit as a platoon commander, and again returned to his battalion on the northern sector of the Eastern Front near Novgorod. He served as a platoon commander with both 1 and 3 Kompanie of the battalion, subsequently moving to the central sector of the Front and seeing action at the great defensive battle at Velikie Luki. In mid 1943 Leutnant Keese attended a company commander's training course and on his return he was appointed battalion adjutant. The battalion moved yet again, to the southern sector of the Front, and saw fierce fighting in the battle for Kiev, where it suffered heavy casualties. The combat engineers of Keese's battalion were always to be found in the thick of the fighting, acquitting themselves with great distinction. On 1 January 1944 he was promoted to Oberleutnant and shortly afterwards was decorated with the German Cross in Gold for his personal gallantry and leadership during the winter battles of 1943. Oberleutnant Keese was appointed company commander of 2 Kompanie.

The entire 20th Panzer Grenadier Division was severely mauled during the great Soviet offensive in the summer of 1944. Once again the combat engineers were in the thick of the fighting, enhancing their already high reputation for fearlessness in the attack and steadfastness in defence. The personal examples of gallantry and dedication shown by Keese were a great inspiration to his men. On 27 July his name was added to the Roll of Honour of the German Army in recognition of this, and on 1 August he was promoted to Hauptmann.

The tide by now having irreversibly turned against the Germans in the east, 20th Panzer Grenadier Division was pushed ever westward. At Orel, at Kiev, the Dnieper, the Tarnopol cauldron and Berditschew,

– at every major battle along the line of retreat, the Pioniere fought with exemplary courage and determination. On many occasions Hauptmann Keese displayed conspicuous gallantry in the face of the enemy. Always in the thick of the fighting, he showed little concern for his own safety despite overwhelming enemy superiority, and inspired his troops by his own example. For continued acts of gallantry during the defensive battles in the summer and autumn of 1944 Hauptmann Keese was decorated with the Knight's Cross of the Iron Cross on 20 October 1944.

On 20 November 1944 Keese was assigned to a battalion commanders' course at the Pionierschule at Dessau and on successful completion of this he was appointed commander of his old unit, Pionier Bataillon 20 on 16 December 1944. Keese commanded the battalion during the retreat through southern Poland, Silesia and the crossing of the Oder near Weisswasser. In March 1945, the remnant of this once powerful division were ordered to proceed to Berlin and assist in the defence of the city. Horrified at this prospect, which he knew meant certain annihilation, the divisional commander, General Scholz, committed suicide. Keese and his men followed their orders however, and took part in the defence of the Seelow heights near Berlin before retreating into the city itself. Here in the rubble of the once proud capital of the Third Reich, Keese and his Pioniere proved themselves adept at making the advancing enemy pay dearly for every yard. On 28 March 1945 Keese became the 805th soldier of the German Wehrmacht to win the Oakleaves to the Knight's Cross of the Iron Cross and was also promoted to the rank of Major. On 22 April Keese was severely wounded during fierce fighting at the Underground station at Berlin-Köpenick. Taken to hospital at Berlin-Döberitz, he was eventually evacuated by fishing boat from Schwerin reaching, after fourteen days, a temporary hospital set up in a school in Schleswig-Holstein. He thus escaped Soviet captivity and was captured by the British. He was released in December 1945.

After the war, Keese worked for the Elektrizitätswerk Wesertal and its offshoots until he retired in 1981. Among the other military decorations won by this gallant soldier were the Close Combat Badge for hand-to-hand fighting, in both Bronze and Silver, and the Wound Badge in Gold.

1945

With his final great offensive utterly defeated, more than 120,000 men and 600 tanks lost, Hitler could only watch in fury as his crumbling Wehrmacht was relentlessly pushed back on all fronts. Both Eastern and Western Allies pushed deep into the Reich itself. German troops became increasingly disheartened and even Hitler's favourite Waffen-SS troops became reluctant to squander their lives in pointless last-ditch actions. This was not to say, however, that these men did not fight bravely when the situation demanded it, merely that they were reluctant to throw away their lives for no good reason when the war was obviously lost and the end was imminent.

Even at this stage, however, the German soldier was capable of showing amazing fortitude and on many occasions the retreating German armies turned and gave their pursuers a bloody nose and cause to treat the battered Wehrmacht with cautious respect. Several cut-off pockets of resistance held out until the very last day of the war. Even as the Russians stalked the streets of Berlin, individual German soldiers displayed outstanding courage, tackling Russian heavy tanks with little more than their bare hands. Knight's Crosses were being awarded direct from the *Reichskanzlei* to the last moments of the war, and thereafter by the short-lived Dönitz regime after Hitler's death.

In 1945 a total of 1,147 Knight's Crosses were awarded, the largest proportion, some 312 awards, being made in April. A total of 192 Oakleaves and 41 Swords were also awarded in the last five months of the war. The German Army and Waffen-SS had won a total of approximately 4,962 from a total of nearly 7,000 Knight's Crosses awarded during the entire war. In addition, a proportion of the Luftwaffe's share of 1,716 awards was to paratroopers and men of the Hermann Göring Panzer Korps fighting in the field.

Oberleutnant Rudolf Donth

Rudolf Donth was born on 16 February 1920 in Schreiberhau, Silesia. His military career began on 1 October 1939 when he was called up for service in the Luftwaffe. He joined Luftwaffe Bau Bataillon Schweichitz in Silesia for six months before transferring to Luftwaffe Ausbildungs Regiment Döberitz.

In the summer of 1940 Donth began his paratroop training at Wittstock before being posted to the Staff Company of Fallschirmjäger Regiment 3 where he was promoted to Gefreiter in November 1940 during which month he also qualified for his paratrooper wings. The recently formed regiment was part of 7 Flieger Division, Germany's original paratroop division.

During 1941 Donth took part in the air assault of Crete when 7 Flieger Division played the major part in the defeat of General Freyberg's Allied Expeditionary Force. Although the Fallschirmjäger played the major role, they did in fact number only some 8,000 from a total German force of about 22,000. German Intelligence had estimated an Allied garrison of about 5,000 men, but the Expeditionary Force in fact numbered almost 42,000. In the fierce combat which ensued the German paras gained a reputation for gallantry and fierce determination which became almost legendary and established themselves as one of the world's great élite forces. While the battle for Crete was conducted with a reasonable degree of chivalry which left both sides with a healthy respect for the soldierly qualities of the other, incidents such as the slaughter and mutilation of more than 130 German wounded by Cretan partisans was a sinister forerunner of the sort of savagery which would soon become all too familiar.

Fallschirmjäger Regiment 3 was tasked with the capture of Galatas, Canea and Suda Bay. I Bataillon was dropped straight into New Zealand infantry positions and was almost completely wiped out. I and II Bataillon troops captured Agya Prison which was put into use as a Regimental HQ. On 21 May Maleme fell to the Germans and just six days later the evacuation of the Allied forces was ordered. On the following day Heraklion was lost to the Germans and the Allies fell back to positions to the east of Fallschirmjäger Regiment 3's target at Suda Bay whence, by the last day of the month, the remaining Allied troops had been evacuated. High German casualties, however, caused Hitler to insist that such large-scale parachute operations never be used again, and henceforth Donth and his comrades found themselves increasingly being used as infantry, albeit élite infantry. Transferred to the northern sector of the Eastern Front, Donth served during the drive towards Leningrad. He saw action at Rzhev and Mius where his gallantry under fire earned him the Iron Cross Second Class on 12 June and the First Class just ten days later.

On 1 October 1942 Donth was transferred to 2 Kompanie of the Fallschirmjäger Ski Bataillon as a section leader with promotion to the rank of Oberjäger. He served with this unit for six months until April

1943. Reorganization of the original 7 Flieger Division had produced a new formation, 1 Fallschirm Division, under Generalmajor Richard Heidrich, himself a veteran of Crete and the battle of Leningrad. Donth joined the division in France where it was forming up and undergoing intensive training. He remained a section leader, but this time with 6 Kompanie of Fallschirmjäger Regiment 4. At about this time Donth was presented with his Kreta Cufftitle, introduced in late 1942 for all those who had participated in the battle for Crete.

In July 1943 the regiment moved to Sicily and was involved in fierce rearguard actions after the Allied invasion, delaying the enemy drive on the Catania Plain. The division was involved in furious combat with British paras at the Primasole Bridge and indeed Fallschirmjäger were among the very last troops to be evacuated to the Italian mainland. Here, 1 Fallschirm Division was engaged in bitter contest with Montgomery's Eighth Army at Foggia. In early 1944 the division found itself committed to what was to become one of the greatest battles of the war, that for Monte Cassino where once again the Fallschirmjäger proved themselves some of the toughest troops in the world. During this hectic struggle Donth was wounded in action for the first time, receiving the Wound Badge in Black. In March he qualified for the Ground Combat Badge of the Luftwaffe and on 1 April 1944 was promoted to Feldwebel.

Massive Allied air raids had levelled the town of Cassino and Allied armour found great difficulty operating in the rubble. Indeed on 22 April Donth was awarded the badge for single-handed destruction of an enemy tank. This badge was awarded only to those who had personally destroyed an enemy tank with hand-held weapons such as grenades, satchel-charges, etc. Despite being greatly outnumbered, the advantageous defensive positions occupied by the Fallschirmjäger allowed them to defeat all Allied attempts to dislodge them. Only in late May after the Cassino flank defences had been breached and the Fallschirmjäger were in danger of being cut off were they finally withdrawn, unbeaten in battle.

June 1944 saw Donth and his comrades in the mountains to the north of Florence defending part of the Gothic Line. The division was made responsible for defending the Futa Pass, and clashed head-on with US Fifth Army while Montgomery's Eighth Army attacked its eastern flank. With the advantage of height and well dug-in positions, the paras were able to put up a highly effective defence. By September, however, sheer weight of numbers began to tell and the German defences began to give way. In late October, Fallschirmjäger Regiment 4 was located at the bridgehead south of Savio. As a 24-year-old sergeant, Donth had command of 6 Kompanie, defending a supply route which crossed a river bend at that location. This was quite a high level of responsibility for a soldier of that rank, but Donth's regimental commander had full confidence in his abilities as one of his most experienced soldiers. Near Orsogna, as NCO in charge of a reconnaissance mission with one other soldier, behind enemy lines, he had positioned himself on the roof of a house containing a British Regimental HQ and for thirty-eight hours had monitored and reported back vital information. Such amazing, cool-headed behaviour in such a situation clearly indicated that here was a man with nerves of steel who could be depended upon in the most adverse conditions.

Now Donth and his 6 Kompanie came under attack by enemy troops in battalion strength with ten tanks in support. Shortly afterwards, units on his flanks also came under attack and a minor breakthrough to a depth of about one kilometre was achieved. Donth's positions came under a heavy creeping barrage of artillery fire behind cover of which a large force with tank support was approaching. As the attackers reached his positions, Donth rallied his men and, despite being heavily outnumbered, led a counter-attack of such ferocity that six enemy tanks were destroyed and its infantry badly battered. Donth even succeeded in freeing some wounded paras who had been taken prisoner by the enemy. Four weeks later, in an action near Bologna, Donth assembled a small assault group and without the advantage of any artillery bombardment to soften-up the enemy, stormed into the opposing British positions, taking eighty-one prisoners including three officers and capturing the entire weapons of two heavy companies. During December 1944 Donth led a platoon-strength night assault with such ferocity that a battalion-strength British unit was thrown out of its positions. Such gallantry did not go unrewarded and on 14 January 1945 Feldwebel Donth was decorated with the Knight's Cross of the Iron Cross. Although a Feldwebel at the time of his award, Donth was commissioned Leutnant with seniority backdated to 1 September 1944.

In April 1945, as the war drew to a close, Donth was assigned to the leadership school of 1 Fallschirm Korps and was promoted Oberleutnant on 20 April. On 2 May Donth was taken into captivity, being released in April 1946.

This, however, was by no means the end of this fine soldier's distinguished career. With the war in Europe barely over, the Cold War began and as the new spheres of influences both east and west became clear, the Western Allies were not long in appreciating that a re-armed West Germany would be a very useful ally. Clearly, Germany was the most likely battlefield in any future war and West German military forces would constitute a valuable element of the West's defences. Donth joined Germany's new armed forces, the Bundeswehr, in September 1956 and retained his former rank of Oberleutnant. Within three months he had requalified for his jump wings with both the Bundeswehr and US Forces at the US 11th Airborne Division in Augsburg.

In May 1957 Donth was promoted to Hauptmann and served as commander of 1 Kompanie, Fallschirmjäger Bataillon 251. He then undertook a number of qualification courses over the next few years including, company commanders' course with the Hammelburg Infantry School, supply officers' course, staff officer training, tactics instructor and aircraft loading specialist. In August 1963, Hauptmann Donth qualified for his para wings with the French Armed Forces, before, during the following month, being trained at the French Special Forces School at Perpignan. On completion of this specialist training he was promoted to Major. Already a highly qualified soldier, Donth then went on to take specialist courses in Psychological Warfare and in April 1966 attended a NATO senior officers' course at the US Special Weapons School. On 3 June 1971 Donth was promoted to Oberstleutnant and went on to become Staff Officer for Reservists in Verteidigungs Bezirks Kommando 61 (Augsburg).

Oberstleutnant Donth finally retired in April 1977. In a military career of 27 years, Donth had seen action at some of history's greatest battles, earned one of his country's highest awards for valour and then gone on post-war to become a highly qualified para officer and serve his country well in peace as well as war.

Today, in retirement, Rudolf Donth retains his connection to the élite paras as the Archivist of the Bund Deutscher Fallschirmjäger.

⁓ Oberstleutnant Paul Liebing

Born on 12 August 1912 in Dresden, Paul Liebing joined the Polizei in April 1932 and was trained at the Polizeischule in Meissen. In September of the following year he attended further training, becoming a Polizei officer candidate. On successful completion of the course he was promoted to Fähnrich in August 1934. In February 1935, Liebing became a machine-gun section leader in the Polizei Macshinengewehr Kompanie in Dresden. April saw Liebing attend a course at the Munich Riding School for mounted police officers on his being commissioned Leutnant der Landespolizei.

In the autumn of 1935 Liebing was transferred to the Luftwaffe, retaining his rank of Leutnant, and was posted to the staff of the Pilots' School in Celle. In March 1937 he began his own flying training in Brunswick, qualifying for his pilot's wings in June 1937. One month later he was promoted to Oberleutnant. Two months after the outbreak of war, Oberleutnant Liebing was posted to Aufklärer Schule 2, before, in April 1940, attending a course for Squadron Leaders. In June he joined 4(H) Aufklärungsgruppe 31 as a reconnaissance pilot, serving in that capacity during the assault on France and the Low Countries with sufficient distinction to win the Iron Cross Second Class for his proficiency. He was promoted to Hauptmann on 1 July 1940.

By 1941 Liebing was a squadron leader in a reconnaissance unit operating from Finland. On 14 June he qualified for the Reconnaissance Flight Clasp in Bronze and in September was awarded the Iron Cross First Class for completing a considerable number of successful reconnaissance missions over enemy territory. In 1942 the Luftwaffe gained its first field divisions. These were, frankly, little more than the result of Hermann Göring's monstrous egotism. Not content with his Air Force and his own Hermann Göring Division, he sought to curry favour and increase his personal influence by raising a number of combat units from existing Luftwaffe manpower which could be committed to the great battle in the east.

Assembled from a motley collection of ground crew, instructors, air crew, air traffic controllers and others, most of whom had little or no combat experience, they received totally inadequate training before being committed to battle and achieved very mixed results. The quality of some of these units was quite poor while others fought reasonably well. This was no fault of the individual soldiers some of whom, like Liebing, went on to be highly decorated, but rather of the Luftwaffe hierarchy which sought to use these men in tasks for which they were ill suited.

Liebing found himself posted to 1 Luftwaffe Feld Division in September 1942, becoming a platoon commander in a Reconnaissance unit. He was promoted to Major in February 1943, becoming company commander, and served on the northern sector of the Eastern Front near Leningrad. The division suffered heavy casualties during the Russian counter-offensives. At the end of October 1943, Major Liebing was transferred to the Officer Reserve of the Commander-in-Chief of the Luftwaffe, and after six months in the Reserves he was posted to the Officer Training School in Nancy, occupied France, where his combat experience on the Eastern Front was put to good use when he became a tactics instructor.

Just one month later, however, the call of duty saw Liebing once again given a combat posting when he became a battalion commander in 6 Fallschirm Division. The division was formed in northern France and was quickly thrown into battle following the Allied landings in Normandy, suffering heavy casualties fighting in the area around Amiens. Even the tough paras could only achieve so much against the overwhelming superiority in numbers boasted by the Allies. Their control of the skies meant that the division could only safely move at night. Any vehicles moving in daylight would soon fall victim to Allied fighter-bombers. The division was then further weakened by the loss of Fallschirmjäger Regiment 16 which was sent to reinforce the Hermann Göring Division on the Eastern Front. The remains were then split up into Kampfgruppen which conducted a fighting withdrawal into Holland. Major Liebing served with Kampfgruppe Eggersch and saw action during the Allied airborne attack at Arnhem and also at Nijmegen.

In November 1944, Liebing took command of Fallschirmjäger Regiment 23 in 2 Fallschirm Division. On 1 March 1945 he was tasked to defend the area near Krefeld with his regiment. Just one day later, the Allies succeeded in breaking through the German lines defended by Liebing's neighbouring unit, 15th Panzer Grenadier Division. The area occupied by II Bataillon of Liebing's regiment was in danger of being encircled as the enemy approached the battalion's HQ positions. On the evening of the same day, Liebing himself led a furious counter-attack, tearing into the flanks of the advancing Allied forces and linking up with the troops of II Bataillon. No sooner had this been achieved than he was ordered to Uerdingen where German pioneers had failed to blow the strategically important bridge. Each time the charges had been set the fuzes had been shot away by enemy fire. Now Liebing was tasked to take his regiment and form a small bridgehead on the west bank. Here he was to hold back the enemy until the troops of the Panzer Lehr Division could build their defensive positions at Rheinhausen. Then Leibing was to blow the bridge and escape with his men by boat to the east bank.

In the afternoon of 3 March the enemy was massing some 500 metres south of the bridge. Some 50 enemy tanks plus supporting infantry were preparing to attack. Liebing's Fallschirmjäger were no longer the tough veterans of battles such as Crete or Cassino, most of whom had long since perished. Now the much enlarged paratroop forces available to Germany were padded out with conscripted troops of all sorts, some of whom had had inadequate training. There were, however, sufficient numbers of veterans in the division's cadre to stiffen the morale of the newer men, all of whom were well aware of what was expected of them as élite troops. The Allied assault soon broke with fury on the defenders of the bridge. Attack after attack was launched, but each was rebuffed by the gallant paras. Despite artillery bombardments and heavy tank fire, the defenders could not be dislodged.

Constantly encouraging his men to greater efforts, Liebing's total disregard for his own safety brought him the absolute trust of his men who responded with ever greater determination. In fact, they held the bridge against overwhelming odds until the morning of the following day, when Liebing blew the bridge. He had far exceeded what had been expected of him, but even now he refused to abandon his heavy weapons and equipment and escape across the river in the small boats which had been assembled. Instead, Liebing gathered his depleted force and, striking north, broke through the encircling Allied forces towards Friemersheim. Liebing's personal gallantry in the bitter fighting of this breakout was an inspiration to his men. Eventually reaching the defences of Rheinhausen, his force of Fallschirmjäger was a very welcome addition to the power available to the defenders and allowed them to hold back the advancing Allies considerably longer than would otherwise have been possible. Liebing and his men subsequently fought at the Homberg bridgehead where once again the gallantry shown by this much depleted group of paras was instrumental in rebuffing several Allied assaults before the Homberg Bridge was blown and he escaped over the Rhine with his men.

On 2 April 1945 Major Liebing was decorated with the Knight's Cross of the Iron Cross in recognition of the great achievements brought about by his personal gallantry and inspired leadership of the men of Fallschirmjäger Regiment 23. On 20 April Liebing was given a richly deserved promotion to Oberstleutnant. Just six days later he was captured by the Americans. His war was over.

SS-Standartenjunker Willi Fey

Willi Fey was born on 25 September 1918, the son of a craftsman in Giessen. After attending Volksschule from 1924 to 1932 Fey became a confectioner and, indeed, in 1939, the 19-year-old Fey became a qualified Master Confectioner.

His military career began in August 1939 when he joined Infanterie Panzerabwehr Ersatzkompanie 9 in Giessen. Following completion of his training he joined the army's 52 Infanterie Division in Panzerjägerabteilung 52. As an anti-tank gunner he served with distinction in 52 Infanterie Division during the attack on France and the Low Countries, and on 15 June 1940 became the first soldier of his Abteilung to win the Iron Cross Second Class. It was awarded personally by the divisional commander, Generalleutnant Jurgen von Arnim.

In the summer of 1941 52 Infanterie Division was part of the German attack on the Soviet Union, serving as part of Heeresgruppe Mitte taking part in the drive to Moscow. In December 1941 Fey was wounded for the first time during this advance and had to be evacuated to Vienna for hospital treatment and did not return to action until August 1942. Just one month later he was wounded again in fierce fighting near Serpuschow. In furious hand-to-hand fighting over several days non-stop, Fey once again came to the notice of his superiors for his resolute determination in battle. He was decorated with the Iron Cross First Class, as well as the Infantry Assault Badge and Close Combat Clasp in Bronze. At about this time he was also promoted to Unteroffizier.

During the Russian counter-offensive of spring 1943, the division was severely battered in the battle for Smolensk. Once again Fey was wounded and evacuated for hospital treatment in the Reserve Hospital in Magdeburg. While he was in hospital recovering from his wounds, 52 Infanterie Division had become so seriously weakened by its losses that it was decided not to reinforce it and rebuild its strength, but to strip it of many of its essential sub-units and convert it to a so-called Security Division.

On recovery from his wounds, Fey transferred to the Waffen-SS. Following extensive training as a panzer soldier, he was posted to the recently formed schwere SS Panzer Abteilung 102, equipped with the formidable Tiger tank. As a tank commander, Fey saw combat with his Tiger on the Normandy front. Here he achieved great success. On 8 August 1944 in a single day's combat, Fey was able to destroy fifteen M4 Sherman tanks and disable a further seven, along with a number of armoured cars and other vehicles.

As often happened when a single massive Tiger was stalking numerically superior enemy units, the Germans found themselves gradually overwhelmed by sheer weight of numbers and eventually disabled. Fey's Abteilung Commander, SS-Obersturmbannführer Weiss, ordered him over the radio to destroy his Tiger to prevent its capture and escape with his crew on foot. Fey refused to countenance defeat and continued to fight on until, under cover of darkness, three other Tigers from the Abteilung were able to approach and tow his damaged tank to safety. For his gallantry in action and success in destroying enemy tanks, Fey was recommended for the German Cross in Gold and this was duly approved, the award being made on 15 September 1944, by the Commander of II SS Panzer Korps, SS-Obergruppenführer Willi Bittrich.

During the breakout through the Falaise Gap, the Abteilung was battered by countless Allied naval bombardments, fighter-bomber attacks and sheer overwhelming weight of numbers until virtually all its tanks were destroyed or disabled. The surviving crew were reduced from their élite status of panzer men to footslogging infantry. During this period, on foot and with only hand-held weapons, Fey personally destroyed four M4 Shermans, being wounded for the fifth time in the process, and qualifying for the Wound Badge in Gold.

From October 1944 to the end of January 1945 Fey attended a course for panzer officer candidates in Königsbrück before being posted to the SS Panzer Ausbildungs und Ersatz Regiment at

Paderborn. In March 1945 he received his posting order returning him to his unit, now renumbered schwere SS Panzer Abteilung 502, located on the Oder Front. The train carrying him to the Front, however, was halted in Kassel and all soldiers on board formed into an emergency combat group to defend the area around Marburg from an imminent American attack. In command of a group of some thirty or so Labour Corps personnel armed only with small arms and a few Panzerfaust single-shot anti-tank weapons, Fey was tasked to halt an armoured attack over the Ohm near Kirchheim. On the morning of 28 March as dawn broke, the first enemy tanks appeared and clattered on to the bridge. Fey waited until two tanks were on the bridge before opening fire and rapidly disabled both with Panzerfausts. The route over the Ohm was effectively blocked by the disabled tanks.

Narrowly evading capture just two days later, Fey retreated east and eventually reached Berlin, reporting to a collection point at the Air Ministry. Here he was given command of a tank-hunting group assembled from various soldiers from 11 SS-Freiwilligen Panzer Grenadier Division Nordland and French volunteers from 33 Waffen Grenadier Division der SS Charlemagne. In addition there were a number of fanatical Hitler Youth. From 22 to 29 April in the battle for central Berlin, Fey's *ad hoc* combat group made the Russian's pay dearly for each yard they advanced, the streets being littered with knocked-out enemy tanks. Fey personally accounted for eight T-34s bringing his total of enemy tanks destroyed in close combat to fourteen and bringing him two Gold and four Silver tank destruction badges. Kampfgruppe Mohnke immediately applied for the award of the Knight's Cross for this fearless tank hunter. The award was approved and Fey became one of the last recipients of the Knight's Cross in the Second World War.

Willi Fey survived the war and went on to serve as a panzer soldier of the West German Bundeswehr, reaching the rank of Hauptmann. He became a senior official of the *Ordensgemeinschaft der Ritterkreuzträger* and is the author of *Panzer in Brennpunkt der Fronten* and *Panzer Kommandanten Bericht*.

SS-Sturmbannführer Friedrich Richter

Friedrich Richter was born on 9 May 1911 and commenced his distinguished military career in May 1934 when he was accepted into the premier unit of the SS, the Leibstandarte SS Adolf Hitler in Berlin–Lichterfelde. He entered the SS with five years' service in the police under his belt and this experience soon saw him commissioned as an SS-Untersturmführer and platoon commander in 8 (Maschinengewehr) Kompanie. On 10 March 1935 he was promoted to SS-

Obersturmführer. In 1937 his eight years of police and military experience was put to good use when he became an instructor at the SS-Junkerschule Braunschweig. Subsequently he became a weapons instructor with SS-Standarte Germania in Arolsen and Hamburg. Richter was promoted to SS-Hauptsturmführer on 9 November 1939.

Richter saw his first fighting during the French Campaign where he served as Divisional Supply Officer in the SS-Verfügungsdivision. On 10 May the division, under the command of one of the finest SS field commanders, SS-Gruppenführer Paul Hausser, crossed the Meuse, pushing through crumbling Dutch resistance, towards Moerdjk and Rotterdam. On 11 May the division ran into the French Seventh Army. Working alongside the army's 9th Panzer Division, the SS-Verfügungsdivision smashed the French troops and within three days the French Army had withdrawn into Belgium. By late May the SS troops had crossed the Aa Canal and stood just thirty miles from Dunkirk. For his part in the success of the Verfügungsdivision during the Campaign in the West, Hauptsturmführer Richter was awarded the Iron Cross Second Class on 25 July 1940.

The division was disolved shortly after the conclusion of the French Campaign, and its units used to form experienced cadres for new SS formations. The bulk of the personnel, including Richter, went into the new SS Division Reich, later to become the 2nd SS Panzer Division Das Reich. Richter was a company commander with 14 Kompanie of SS-Regiment Deutschland. In July and August of 1941 Richter and his company served on the central sector of the Eastern Front following the invasion of the Soviet Union. The division moved south during September and October, seeing fierce combat at Kiev, Makoschin, Pratschi, Itschna and Romny. Richter's Grenadiers fought with skill and determination during these battles, greatly enhancing its fighting reputation. From October through the winter, the Reich Division moved back to the central sector of the Front, taking part in the drive to Moscow and reaching to within 16 kilometres of the Soviet capital city. Richter was decorated with the Iron Cross First Class for his part in these winter battles. The division had by now fully justified its élite status by its superb fighting record. This was only gained at considerable cost, however. The division lost some 60 per cent of its combat strength during the horrors of that first winter campaign; more than 10,000 young SS Grenadiers were dead from this division alone.

In February 1942 SS-Hauptsturmführer Richter was posted to the Kraftfahrtechnische Lehranstalt in Vienna. In March, he was posted to the Fallingbostel training grounds where he involved himself with the recruitment and training of new junior NCOs for the division which was to be withdrawn from the Front for rest and refit. The division moved to France where it was completely rebuilt, expanded and upgraded to the status of a panzer division and its title slightly altered, from Reich to Das Reich. Richter attended the panzer gunnery school in Putlos and the panzer research institute in Berlin.

In January 1943 Richter returned to the Eastern Front, as commander of 5 Kompanie SS-Regiment Deutschland, taking part in the great battle for Kharkov where he was wounded for the first time, earning the Wound Badge in Black. From February to May he was hospitalized to recover from his wounds. On his recovery he was involved in setting up a 'convalescent Company' for wounded soldiers of Panzer Korps Hausser at Pessotschin near Kharkov. Richter took charge of the Field Replacement Battalion of the 2nd SS Panzer Division.

As commander of the rearguard during the retreat over the Dnieper he led III Bataillon of the SS-Regiment Der Führer in ferocious combat at Poltawa where the SS men made the enemy pay dearly for every yard of their advance. In November 1944 he was posted to the SS-Junkerschule at Bad Tölz in Bavaria where he served as a tactics instructor until May 1944 when he was posted to the Artillerieschule at Beneschau in Czechoslovakia as an instructor in tactics.

In July 1944 Richter was appointed batallion commander of I Bataillon, SS-Panzer Grenadier Regiment 22, in 10th SS Panzer Division Frundsberg. The division was severely mauled in the Normandy fighting and was cut off in the Falaise pocket, losing much of its strength in breaking out. By August this once powerful panzer division had lost all its tanks and was reduced to mere batallion strength. It withdrew into Holland and was sent to rest and refit in a peaceful area – Arnhem!

Frundesberg was by no means up to strength when the British paratroops landed at Arnhem; indeed much of the German strength was split into small battle groups. Richter commanded such a Kampfgruppe, part of Fallschirmjäger Gruppe Walther. Once the British threat to Arnhem had been eliminated, Frundsberg served as part of Generaloberst Student's 1 Fallschirm Armee in the battles around the Albert Canal. From October to December Richter commanded the Kampfschule at Goor in Holland, training junior NCOs and assault troop leaders. In November 1944 Friedrich Richter was promoted to SS-Sturmbannführer.

By early February 1945 Richter was in Pommerania, commanding III Bataillon, SS Panzer Grenadier Regiment 21. The regiment fought doggedly but in vain, as the overwhelming strength of the Russians pushed the Germans steadily westwards, into the heart of the Reich. On 4 March Richter was tasked to defend the line Hohenschönau – Küss – Grosse Sabow against the enemy advance. The Russians had reached Wilhelmfelde, 1.5 kilometres east of Naugard with considerable strength in both tanks and infantry. Richter gathered all available forces south of Naugard and formed a defence for his endangered right flank. When the massed enemy attack finally fell upon his meagre forces, Richter's Grenadiers put up a stout defence, knocking out twelve enemy tanks with Panzerfausts, and throwing back two powerful enemy assaults. By his determination, personal fearlessness and undoubted gallantry in the face of the enemy, Richter had shown exemplary conduct despite being wounded himself. He prevented the enemy breakthrough at Naugard and protected the essential supply route of the Naugard–Gollnow highway. This delay to the Russian advance allowed the rest of the division to build a much stronger defensive position. A personal covering letter to a recommendation for the Knight's Cross for Richter, written by Waffen-SS Panzer General Heinz Harmel, shows the high regard in which Richter was held:

'10 SS Panzer Division Frundsberg
SS-Sturmbannführer Richter is known to me personally as a brave battalion commander from many actions. His independent, daring determination, to take his Kampfgruppe into the dangerous positions south of Naugard, not only gave the SS-Panzer Grenadier Regiment 21 time to organize a defensive front, but was also of decisive importance for the defence of the flanks of the main force.
I particularly advocate the award of the Knight's Cross of the Iron Cross for this daring officer.

The Divisional Commander
signed Harmel
SS-Brigadeführer and Major-General
of the Waffen-SS.'

Richter was awarded the Knight's Cross on 6 May 1945.

After being wounded, Richter was taken to hospital in Magdeburg. Attached to the staff of Armeegruppe Steiner, Richter fled west at the capitulation to avoid Russian captivity. On 2 May he was taken prisoner by the Americans but escaped en route to a prisoner-of-war camp. Under a false identity, he was eventually interned by the Americans. Along with many of his Waffen-SS comrades Richter preferred to go 'underground' and live under a false name rather than risk identification as an SS officer. The Allies were not exactly inclined to feel any sympathy for former SS soldiers and made little or no differentiation between their treatment of honest fighting soldiers and the dregs of the SS who staffed the concentration camps. Eventually, however, he was discovered and taken to the camp in Fallingbostel run by the Allied Secret Service units. He suffered solitary confinement and intensive interrogations before the Allies finally accepted his status as a true combat soldier with no stain on his character and he was duly released.

Friedrich Richter subsequently lived quietly in retirement until his death in 1990.

SS-Obersturmführer Gustav-Peter Reber

Born in Leimen on 5 June 1919, Gustav-Peter Reber joined the SS-Verfügungstruppe on 1 November 1938 when he became a member of the élite Liebstandarte SS Adolf Hitler in Berlin. With the Leibstandarte Reber served during the occupation of the Sudetenland and gained combat experience during the Polish Campaign and the attack on France and the Low Countries.

After the fall of France the Leibstandarte was moved south into the Balkans and played an important part in the invasion of Greece. Reber took part in the audacious storming and capture of the Klidi Pass in April 1941 and was wounded in action, earning himself a promotion to SS-Unterscharführer and the award of the Iron Cross Second Class. On recovery from his wounds he was posted to 'V' Bataillon of the Leibstandarte in Berlin where he remained until February 1942 when the battalion was flown into the northern sector of the Eastern Front to take part in the assault on Leningrad. On the night of 12/13 March Reber led an assault group in an attack on an enemy trench system. In 56 degrees of frost, the SS Grenadiers stormed forward, clearing the trenches and bunkers with hand-grenades and machine pistols. Many prisoners were taken and Reber was again wounded. For his part in the action he was rewarded with the Iron Cross First Class.

The Leibstandarte troops were then pulled out of the line and moved to France for rest and refitting. At this time it was also upgraded and renamed 1st SS Panzer Grenadier Division Leibstandarte SS Adolf Hitler. Much expanded and reinforced, it returned to the Eastern Front in the spring of 1943 and gained a first-class fighting reputation at the battles of Kharkov, Kursk and Bjelgorod. Here, Reber distinguished himsef once again. He and his section had been tasked to spearhead an assault on enemy positions on Hill 812. In a determined attack under heavy defensive fire, Reber and his men stormed forwards with only small arms and hand-grenades and determinedly made their way up the hill. Only Reber and two of his comrades reached the top, the remainder having fallen to enemy fire. The objective was captured, however, and many prisoners taken. Due to Reber's capture of Hill 812, the Germans were able to pass this strategic defence point totally unmolested by enemy fire. For this achievement and his own gallantry under fire, he was awarded the German Cross in Gold and given a battlefield promotion to SS-Oberscharführer.

On 12 July 1943 during the tank battles around Prochorowka, Reber was once again severely wounded – for the sixth time – and was evacuated to Germany. On his recovery, he was selected for officer training and sent to the SS-Junkerschule Kienschlag and passed out best of course. He was commissioned SS-Untersturmführer in June 1944. Thereafter he was posted to SS XL Armee Korps in Poland where he served as adjutant to SS-Obergruppenführer Matthias Kleinheisterkamp.

From early January 1945 Reber and the corps staff were located at Kustrin on the Oder. On 16 April 1945 a major Russian offensive directed on Berlin began. Corps HQ had to be moved first to Fürstenwalde then two days later to Bad Saarow just as the massed Russian forces broke through the German lines. Reber, in command of the Corps escort troops, quickly gathered his men and with as many other soldiers as he could commandeer formed them into combat groups, launching an immediate counter-attack. Despite heavy losses Reber was able to hold the line until reinforcements arrived and the positions were secured. For his achievement Reber was awarded the Knight's Cross on 28 April 1945.

On the same day, the Russians succeeded in cutting off the German forces around Halbe. On the night of 28/29 April some Tiger tanks of schwere SS Panzer Abteilung 502 with the staff of SS XI Panzer Korps attempted to break out to the west. Reber, with his escort troops and the remainder of the corps staff, was ordered to follow. As he and his men moved through the wooded area he could see vast numbers of refugees who were also seeking to avoid being caught by the Russians. Reber's troops were greatly outnumbered by the enemy and his losses were heavy as the German force ran into the encircling Russians. Hand-to-hand combat ensued and Reber had his machine pistol shot out of his hands. He did not falter, however, and at the head of his men, rallied them forward, finally breaking through the Russian positions with his much weakened force.

Some degree of reinforcement was achieved, however, by linking up with other groups of stragglers. Russian tanks were then encountered, many of which were destroyed by the desperate Germans. Reber personally knocked out two T-34s. His group also saw combat with turncoat German soldiers of the Komitees Freies Deutschland. These were captured German soldiers who for reasons of political belief, expediency, or mere cowardice, had turned traitor and offered to fight against their former comrades. Reber was shot and wounded by one of these men, but helped by comrades, succeeded in reaching and crossing the Elbe.

On 5 May 1945 Gustav Reber finally received the Knight's Cross he had been awarded in April. The award was made by SS-Brigadeführer Jurgen Wagner, using a spare Iron Cross Second Class fitted with a neck ribbon as the chaotic military situation meant that supplies of true Knight's Crosses were unavailable at the Front. More importantly, the entry was made in his personal *Soldbuch*, showing that he had been invested with the decoration. Later on the very same day, Reber was captured by the Russians. Twice on his way to prison camp, he managed to escape briefly, before being recaptured, and then sent to a special punishment camp.

In 1947 Reber was taken before a Soviet tribunal and, unbelievably, accused of being an American spy. Soviet paranoia ensured that he was found guilty and he was sentenced to death, though this was later commuted to 25 years' hard labour. Held in the notorious Workuta labour camp he was forced to work in the mines in temperatures which fell to 60 degrees below zero. His suffering continued until 17 October 1955 when political moves by the West Germans resulted in the release of many prisoners held in the Soviet Union.

Gustav Reber returned to West Germany where he now lives in retirement.

SS-Sturmbannführer Hans Hauser

Hans Hauser was born on 31 January 1916 in Innsbruck and attended both the Volksschule and Bundesoberrealschule there, completing his education in 1935.

At the age of 18, Hauser joined the SS, enlisting in the Nachrichtenstaffel of 8 Kompanie of SS-Standarte Deutschland, based in Munich. From 1 April 1937 to March 1938 he attended the SS-Junkerschule Braunschweig, completing an officer candidate's course and was commissioned as an SS-Untersturmführer and, specializing in police work, became a Polizei Leutnant at the same time. Hauser was posted to Mannheim where he took up his duties as the youngest officer of the unit. He also had the honour of being the unit's standard-bearer.

Between May 1938 and August 1939 Hauser went on to attend further training courses at the Polizeischule in Fürstenfeldbruck before becoming a platoon commander in Polizei-Hundertschaft Mannheim. On 30 January 1940 he was promoted to Oberleutnant. In March 1942 he was assigned to the army where his Polizei experience was put to good use. He became a military police officer with Feldgendarmerie Truppe 498b (mot), seeing service in Sicily and in Libya with the Afrika Korps. In April 1942 he was promoted to Hauptmann.

On 1 October 1942 Hauptmann Hauser was recalled to Germany. As an experienced police officer with front-line experience as well as being a commissioned officer in the SS, his services were required by General der Polizei Wunnenberg for his 4 SS Polizei Division. Hauser acquired the rank of SS-Hauptsturmführer, the direct equivalent of his army rank of Hauptmann. In the SS-Polizei Division he took command of 2 Kompanie of I Bataillon, SS-Polizei Schutzen Regiment 3, located in Debica in Poland.

Hauser and his men went into action on the northern sector of the Eastern Front in February 1943 near Leningrad where, in fierce combat around Szablind, they were involved in hand-to-hand fighting during the course of a counter-attack against a dangerous Russian penetration of the German positions. Hauser received a bullet wound in the right arm during this action and was awarded the Iron Cross Second Class on 17 February as well as qualifying for the Wound Badge in Black. The SS-Polizei Division suffered heavy casualties on the Leningrad Front, fighting around Lake Ilmen, Volkhov and Lake Ladoga and was withdrawn in the spring of 1943. In the Protectorate of Bohemia–Moravia and in Poland it was used for security duties and anti-partisan actions while it rebuilt its strength. The division spent the summer in Greece before moving east again in the autumn to serve in Serbia. By now Hauser had become Commander of II Bataillon of the SS-Polizei Division's Kampfgruppe. In November 1943, the Kampfgruppe was committed in support of the Luftwaffe's field units fighting in the Oranienbaum cauldron, seeing extremely fierce action. By the first days of January 1944 Hauser's battalion was operating along with army units as a 'fire brigade', rushing from emergency point to emergency point as the Russians hammered the area around Babino. Hauser was seriously wounded for the second time on 10 March 1944.

He was posted as commander of Recruit Depot Kurmarck and on 9 November 1944 promoted to SS-Sturmbannführer and Major der Schutzpolizei. By January 1945 the situation on the northern sector of the Front had deteriorated to such an extent that the personnel of the depot had to be pressed into combat service. They were formed into a Kampfgruppe which Hauser took into action near Posen in bitter defensive actions against the inexorable advance of the Red Army. The Kampfgruppe suffered heavy casualties during the retreat to Guben on the Oder. In March 1945 Hauser and his Kampfgruppe were slowly progressing in the direction of Prague via the Beneschau training grounds, finally arriving in the protectorate at the Junkerschule at Keonschlag.

While awaiting further movement orders, Hauser lost many of his men who were requisitioned into the many *ad hoc* combat units being made up. Hauser himself finally received orders from Berlin assigning him as a regimental commander to the Muslim 13 Waffen-Gebirgs - Division der SS Hanschar, with immediate effect. No one, however, could tell Hauser where his new unit was located. Armed with the unit's field post number, Hauser set off for Vienna. When he arrived, however, he had a shock. A Führer-Order or personal order from Hitler himself had decreed that all available troops be gathered into Kampfgruppen for the defence of the Reich. To this end SS-General Felix Steiner was commandeering all troops passing through Vienna. Hauser found himself with all the other officers, NCOs and other ranks at Schönbrunn, his previous orders now cancelled. Hauser was advised that the deteriorating military situation in the east meant that his previous posting to the Hanschar Division was no longer feasible and that he was to organize a Kampfgruppe from the available personnel at Schönbrunn. The men taken from trains arriving in Vienna included those going on, or returning from, leave, the very lightly wounded and those recuperating from injuries. Hauser was lucky in that many of those caught in the trawl were highly experienced combat soldiers and NCOs, many of whom had been highly decorated. At least he had a tough cadre for his new Kampfgruppe. Within a few days he had his Kampfgruppe organized and, albeit armed with only light infantry weapons, ready for action. Equipped with a number of vehicles, also commandeered wherever possible, Hauser and his men set off for the Front in early April. The vehicles, however, were only on loan. At the first sign of action, Hauser and his men were to dismount and proceed on foot, sending the precious vehicles back to Schönbrunn.

Heading east out of Schönbrunn, Hauser's Kampfgruppe passed huge columns of retreating troops, mostly Hungarian, heading towards the Austrian capital. Once passed these fleeing hordes, the roads seemed eerily empty as Kampfgruppe Hauser found itself alone. By this stage of the war, Hauser, like many other front-line soldiers, had developed a healthy sixth sense for impending danger and the alarm bells in his head were ringing loudly – things were far too quiet. Hauser had his men dismount and sent the vehicles back. Just south of his position lay the village of Münchedorf which a quick reconnaissance revealed was clear of enemy and Hauser had his men quickly occupy the village and set up defensive positions.

Hauser's instincts were soon proved correct. No sooner had his men set up their positions when three T-34 tanks appeared. The Russians were unaware of Hauser's force and rashly approached the village without the benefit of infantry cover. As the first T-34 mounted the bridge leading into the village, Hauser ordered his Grenadiers to open fire with their Panzerfaust anti-tank projectiles which soon scored a direct hit and the T-34 was destroyed, neatly blocking the bridge and preventing the other two from approaching any nearer. A furious barrage of fire, coupled with the loss of their leader, soon persuaded the remaining pair of T-34s to withdraw.

Hauser made use of the respite, ordering his men to strengthen their defences as much as possible. Luckily so, as just before midnight a furious barrage of artillery shells and Katyusha rockets fell upon the little village. The Russians were softening-up the Germans before launching a massed infantry attack. Three times in the space of the first hour Hauser's command post was hit and had to be moved to an alternate position. In the bombardment Hauser lost both his adjutant and his orderly officer. A very brief respite followed the bombardment before a renewed attack by T-34s was launched on the village, during which a further T-34 was knocked out by a Panzerfaust.

During the hours of darkness a German Tiger Tank made contact with Hauser's small force. The Germans were delighted at the prospect of the support of the steel leviathan, but unfortunately the tank commander had only come to deliver a message. Hauser's force was located in a dangerous gap between the SS Regiments Der Führer and Deutschland, components of the élite 2nd SS Panzer Division Das Reich. Hauser was given the express order to hold that gap for at least 3 to 4 days so that the Das Reich troops could consolidate their defences. The Tiger then withdrew, much to the dismay of Hauser's Grenadiers, and the small group prepared themselves for the imminent attack they knew must come.

By now Hauser's men had managed to construct fairly strong defensive positions facing the Russians and a further attack by yet more T-34s was successfully rebuffed. The village itself was by now reduced to rubble by continuous bombardments. Clearly, enemy reconnaissance of the village had been very poor. Here was Hauser's Kampf-gruppe armed with only light weapons and his forces concentrated all on the south side of the village facing the enemy. Had the Russians attempted a proper reconnaissance they would have realised how weakly defended the German flanks were and could easily have liquidated the Germans. Instead repeated frontal attacks were made which the Germans, albeit at some cost, were able to rebuff. On the second day, Russian forces did eventually manage to achieve a toehold on the village after furious hand-to-hand fighting with the greatly outnumbered Germans. By the fourth day approximately half the village was in enemy hands and Hauser's losses were such that he was by now barely able to hold off the enemy and was certainly in no condition to expel them from the village. Finally, on the evening of the fourth day, came word from division that Hauser had accomplished his task, the divisional defences were secure and his Kampfgruppe could now withdraw to safety. A much relieved Hauser could now attempt to get his sadly depleted little force back to the German lines. Under cover of darkness he successfully disengaged and managed to get the bulk of his remaining troops to the safety of Der Führer Regiment's positions. Reporting to the regimental commander, SS-Obersturmbannführer

Otto Weidinger, Hauser was given command of I Bataillon of the regiment, its previous commander having just been killed in action. At the same time Weidinger expressed the grateful thanks of the Das Reich Division for the gallantry of Hauser and his men in holding out against overwhelming enemy forces for so long, and advised him that he had been recommended for the Knight's Cross.

Hauser was decorated with the Knight's Cross on 6 May 1945.

Proud to have now joined this élite division, Hauser led his battalion in the vicious hand-to-hand fighting withdrawal by Mödling to the Florisdorfer Bridge in Vienna. On 29 April the Der Führer Regiment was rushed to the area around Dresden where preparations were being made for an attack against the 4th Polish Tank Army in the direction of Berlin. No sooner were they ready, however, than they were withdrawn and rushed to Prague to combat the Czech insurrection. The mere presence of such a powerful unit intimidated the Czechs enough to allow the Waffen-SS troops to escort a huge number of German civilians, female auxiliaries and numerous leaderless units and individuals out of Prague. These unfortunates would almost certainly have perished as did many others in Czech territory when the war ended, as the local populace sought revenge on the hated Germans.

Hauser's regiment withdrew to Rockizan where it surrendered to American troops. It was held by the Americans at Klattau just adjacent to the Soviet zone until September when it was moved to Regensburg. Shortly before Christmas 1945, the officers were separated from the NCOs and other ranks. Due to Hauser having a similar name to the famous SS General Paul Hausser, he was transferred to the prison at Dachau and held with more than one hundred captured German Generals.

Hauser now lives quietly in retirement, and has written the history of the regiment's time in captivity, entitled *Regiment Der Führer, 1945–49*.

APPENDIXES

APPENDIXES

Appendix 1
Comparative Ranks

As far as officer ranks were concerned, most German ranks had a more or less direct equivalent in the British or US Armies. There were a number of NCO ranks, however, which had only a very rough equivalent in the Allied armies. Whereas in the British Army for instance there were two grades of corporal, lance-corporal and full corporal, in the German forces, each rank tended to have its own insignia, thus implying that the Germans had a much wider range of NCO ranks. It should be remembered therefore that only approximate comparisons are shown for NCO ranks.

The term Grenadier has been used to illustrate the rank of private in the German Army. This term could be varied depending on the branch of service, i.e., Schütze, Jäger, etc.

British Army	German Army/ Luftwaffe	German Waffen-SS	US Army
Private	Grenadier	SS-Schutze	Private
	Obergrenadier	SS-Oberschutze	Private 1st Class
Lance-Corporal	Gefreiter	SS-Sturmann	
	Obergefreiter	SS-Rottenführer	
	Stabsgefreiter		
Corporal	Unteroffizier	SS-Unterscharführer	Corporal
Sergeant	Unterfeldwebel	SS-Scharführer	Sergeant
Staff-Sergeant	Feldwebel	SS-Oberscharführer	Staff Sergeant
Warrant Officer Class 2	Oberfeldwebel	SS-Hauptscharführer	Master Sergeant
Warrant Officer Class 1	Stabsfeldwebel	SS-Sturmscharführer	Warrant Officer
Second Lieutenant	Leutnant	SS-Untersturmführer	Second Lieutenant
First Leutenant	Oberleutnant	SS-Obersturmführer	Lieutenant
Captain	Hauptmann	SS-Hauptsturmführer	Captain
Major	Major	SS-Sturmbannführer	Major
Lieutenant-Colonel	Oberstleutnant	SS-Obersturmbannführer	Lieutenant Colonel
Colonel	Oberst	SS-Standartenführer SS-Oberführer	Colonel
Brigadier		SS-Brigadeführer	Brigadier
Major-General	Generalmajor	SS-Gruppenführer	Major General
Lieutenant-General	Generalleutnant		Lieutenant General

British Army	German Army/ Luftwaffe	German Waffen-SS	US Army
General	General	SS-Obergruppenführer	General
	Generaloberst	SS-Oberstgruppenführer	
Field Marshal	Generalfeld-marshall		

Appendix 2
Unit Structure

As a very rough guide to those unfamiliar with the structure of the German military unit during the Second World War, the following shows the approximate structure of a typical infantry unit.

The basic unit was the Infantry Section. A small group of Infantrymen commanded by a Section Leader who would normally be a Sergeant or perhaps a Senior Corporal. A number of such sections would make up a Platoon, which would be commanded by a senior NCO such as a Warrant Officer or junior Officer such as a Second Lieutenant. Several Platoons would make up a Company, probably commanded by a Captain or a Major.

The next larger formation, the Battalion, would be made up of a number of such Companies. By the time a unit of this size is reached, it will be found that a number of ancillary troops such as staff personnel, clerks, etc., are also present. A number of Battalions would form a Regiment, probably commanded by a Colonel, with once again, a fair number of ancillary and support troops present. These Regiments would be part of a parent Division, probably commanded by a Major, General or Lieutenant-General. The Divisions would be grouped together in a Corps, and several Corps in an Army. Armies were grouped together to form an Army Group usually titled after the geographical area – Heeresgruppe Nord (Army Group North) or after the General commanding the group.

A typical Infantry Division would contain three Infantry and one Artillery Regiments, plus, Engineer, Reconaissance, Anti-Tank and Signals Battalions. In addition, were medical troops, clerical personnel, Quartermasters and Military Police, etc.

When written down, the titles of these units were usually abbreviated and expressed with a combination of both arabic and roman numerals. A Company-sized unit is usually seen expressed with an arabic numeral, i.e., 4 Kompanie. A battalion, however, is expressed with a roman numeral, i.e., II Bataillon. These would be shown prefixed to the Regimental designation in which the numeral follows rather than precedes the title, i.e., II Bataillon, Infanterie Regiment 2. This would then be abbreviated thus II / Inf. Rgt. 2. A Division was usually expressed with its numeral preceding the title, and followed by any honour title, i.e., 2 SS-Panzer Division Das Reich.

To express the full designation of a soldier's unit it would be necessary to show his Company or Battalion, Regiment, Division, Corps, Army and Army Group, i.e., 3 Batterie / Sturmgeschütz Abteilung 245 / 260 Infanterie Division / XII Armee Korps / 4. Armee / Heeresgruppe Mitte. This would be abbreviated thus: 3./Stug.Abt.245/260 Inf.Div./XII A.K./4. Armee /H.Gr.Mitte

Glossary

Abwehr — defence, also the name of the German military counter-Intelligence service
Abzeichen — badge, insignia
Abteilung — detachment, battalion-sized military unit
Armee — Army
Armeegruppe — Army Group
Aufklärung — reconnaissance
Aufklärungs-abteilung — reconnaissance detachment
Armee Ober-kommando (AOK) — Army High Command
Artillerie — Artillery
Bataillon — Battalion
Batterie — Battery (of Artillery)
Befehlshaber — commander
Begleit — escort
Brigadeführer — brigade commander (a Waffen-SS rank)
Beobachter — observer
Deutsche Kreuz — German Cross (i.e., the Swastika)
Fahnenjunker — officer cadet
Fähnrich — ensign
Fallschirm-jäger — paratrooper
Flieger — flyer, pilot
Freiwillige — volunteer
Feldwebel — Sergeant
Geschütz — gun, cannon
Heer — Army
Heeresgruppe — Army Group
Infanterie — infantry
Jäger — rifleman
Junkerschule — Military Academy
Kavallerie — Cavalry
Kampf — battle

Kamfgruppe — battle group
Kampfwagen — combat vehicle
Kommando — commando
Komman-dierender General — General Officer in Command
Kompanie — company
Korps — corps
Kradschutzen — motor-cycle infantry
Kraftfahr — motor, motorized
Kriegs-academie — Staff College
Kiegsberichter — war correspondent
Lehr — training
Mitte — centre
Nachrichten — signals
Nahkampf — close-quarter battle, hand-to-hand combat
Oberbefehls-haber — Commander-in-Chief
Ober-kommando — High Command
Oberkom-mando der Wehrmacht (OKW) — High Command of the Armed Forces
Oberkom-mando des Heeres (OKH) — High Command of the Army
Oberkom-mando der Luftwaffe (OKL) — High Command of the Air Force
Ordonnanz Officer — orderly officer
Panzer — armour, tank
Panzerabwehr — anti-tank
Panzer-abwehrkan-none (PAK) — anti-tank gun

Panzer-grenadier	armoured infantry
Panzerjäger	tank destroyer (lit. tank hunter)
Panzer Korps	armoured corps
Pioniere	pioneers, combat engineers
Reichsarbeits-dienst	state labour service
Ritterkreuz	Knight's Cross
Ritterkreuz-träger	Knight's Cross bearer
schwere	heavy
SS-Schutz Staffel	protection squad
SS-Verfüg-ungstruppe (SSVT)	Order troops, the first SS military formations
SS-Verfüngs-division	SS combat unit which evolved into the Das Reich Panzer Division
Stab	staff
Standarte	regimental-sized SS-unit
Sturmge-schütz	self-propelled gun, assault gun
Wacht	watch, guard
Wacht-abteilung	guard detachment
Wacht Offizier	officer of the watch
Waffen-SS	Armed SS, SS military units
Wehrkreis	military district
Wehrmacht	armed forces
Zug	platoon, section
Zugführer	platoon commander, section leader
zBV (zur Besondere Verwen-dung)	for special purposes

Bibliography

Although the bulk of the information required for this book came direct from the soldiers featured themselves, or their surviving relatives where applicable, a number of books were consulted for background information on various units, campaigns, etc. The following books are particularly recommended to any reader who is interested in further studying the subject of the *Ritterkreuzträger* and their military exploits.

Alman, Karl. *Ritterkreuzträger des Afrika Korps*. Erich Pabel Verlag, Rastatt, 1975

Angolia, John R. *On the Field of Honour*, vols 1 and 2. R. J. Bender, San Jose, 1979 and 1980

Bender, Roger J., and Law, Richard D. *Organization, Uniforms and History of the Afrika Korps*. R. J. Bender, San Jose, 1973

Bender, Roger J., and Petersen, George A. *Hermann Göring, from Regiment to Fallschirmpanzerkorps*. R. J. Bender, San Jose, 1975

Deighton, Len. *Blitzkrieg*. Jonathan Cape, London, 1979

Diroll, Bernd. *Die Hamburger Ritterkreuzträger*. Verlag Klaus D. Patzwall, Hamburg, 1984

Edwards, Roger. *German Airborne Troops*. Macdonald & Janes, London, 1974

Kratschmer, Ernst G. *Die Ritterkreuzträger der Waffen-SS*. Verlag K. W. Schutz, Preussische–Oldendorf, 1955

Lenfeld, Erwin, and Thomas, Franz. *Die Eichenlaubträger*. Weilburg Verlag, Wiener Neustadt, 1983

Lucas, James. *Alpine Elite*. Janes Publishing Co Ltd, London, 1980

Luther, Craig. *Blood and Honour*. R. J. Bender, San Jose, 1987

Mitcham, Samuel W. *Hitler's Legions*. Leo Cooper, London, 1985

Möller-Witten, Hans. *Mit dem Eichenlaub zum Ritterkreuz*. Erich Pabel Verlag, Rastatt, 1962

Ott, Alfred. *Die Weissen Spiegel*. Podzum Pallas Verlag, Freidberg

Quarrie, Bruce. *German Airborne Troops, 1939–45*. Osprey Publishing, London, 1983

Scheibert, Horst. *Panzer Grenadier Division Grossdeutschland*. Podzun Verlag, 1977

Schneider, Jost W. *Their Honour was Loyalty*. R. J. Bender, San Jose, 1977

Von Seemen, Gerhard. *Die Ritterkreuzträger*. Podzun Pallas Verlag, Friedberg, 1984

Spaeter, Hellmuth. *Panzerkorps Grossdeutschland*. Podzun Pallas Verlag, Friedberg, 1984

Thomas, Franz, and Wegmann, Günther. *Die Ritterkreuzträger der Deutschen Wehrmacht, 1939–45*. vols 1 and 2, Biblio Verlag, Osnabrück, 1985 and 1986

Windrow, Martin. *Luftwaffe Airborne and Field Units*. Osprey Publishing, London, 1972

Periodicals:
Das Ritterkreuz, Magazine of the Knight's Cross bearers' Association
Der Freiwillige, Magazine for Waffen-SS veterans
Der Landser, Magazine for German Army ex-servicemen
Signal, Wartime German propaganda magazine
Völkischer Beobachter, Wartime German newspaper.

Index

B
Barenthin, Oberst Walther, 76
Bittrich, SS-Obergruppenführer Willi, 129
Bremer, SS-Obersturmbannführer Gerd, 104

D
Dietrich, SS-Oberstgruppenführer Sepp, 85
Donth, Oberleutnant Rudolf, 121–5
Dürr, SS-Unterscharführer Emil, 104–6

F
Fey, SS-Standartenjunker, 129–30
Foltin, Major Ferdinand, 97–100

G
German Army Units:
II Armee Korps, 57
Artillerie Regiment Schwerin, 78
Artillerie Regiment 48, 78, 114
Artillerie Lehr Regiment Juterbog, 78
Führerbegleit Brigade, 82
Führergrenadier Brigade, 82
Fusilier Regiment 12, 72
1 Gebirgs Division, 37–8
Gebirgsjäger Regiment 98, 36, 39, 123
Grenadier Regiment 89, 72
Grenadier Regiment 1128, 39
2 Infanterie Division, 101
5 Infanterie Division, 113
12 Infanterie Division, 72, 114
20 Infanterie Division, 118
23 Infanterie Division, 115
52 Infanterie Division, 128
87 Infanterie Division, 94
123 Infanterie Division, 72
205 Infanterie Division, 117
253 Infanterie Division, 60

356 Infanterie Division, 63
Infanterie Regiment 1, 106
Infanterie Regiment 2, 101
Infanterie Regiment 15, 97
Infanterie Regiment 17, 50
Infanterie Regiment 19, 50, 56
Infanterie Regiment 107, 97
Infanterie Regiment 187, 94–5
Infanterie Regiment 473, 60
Infanterie Regiment 871, 63
Infanterie Regiment (mot) Grossdeutschland, 78–9
Infanterieschule Doberitz, 101
Jagd Panzer Kompanie 1205, 117
Jager Regiment 25, 113
Jager Regiment 28, 109
1 Kavallerie Division, 32
Kavallerie Regiment 13, 30, 66
Kavallerie Regiment 22, 32
Kriegsschule Dresden, 33
Kriegsschule Munich, 81
Panzer Abwehr Abteilung 12, 114
9 Panzer Division, 131
24 Panzer Division, 32
20 Panzer Grenadier Division, 119
90 Panzer Grenadier Division, 112
Panzer Grenadier Division Grossdeutschland, 80, 81
Panzer Grenadier Regiment 26, 32
Panzer Grenadier Regiment 160, 77
Panzer Lehr Division, 127
Panzerjäger Abteilung 12, 114
Panzerjäger Abteilung 23, 115
Panzerjäger Abteilung 52, 128
Panzerjäger Abteilung 205, 117
Panzerjäger Abteilung 1205, 117
Panzerjäger (Sturmgeschutz) Abteilung 1023, 118
III Panzer Korps, 38
Pioniere Bataillon 2, 36
Pioniere Bataillon 20, 118

Pioniere Bataillon 31, 33
Pioniereschule Dessau, 56, 119
Pioniereschule Rehagen-Klausdorf, 33
Pioniereschule Munich, 36
Polizei Offizier Schule Eicke, 48
Polizeischule Brandenburg, 48
Polizeischule Furstenfeldbrück, 136
Polizeischule Meissen, 125
Sturmgeschutz Batterie 640, 78
Sturmgeschutz Brigade Grossdeutschland, 82
Sturmgeschutz Brigade 9122, 117

H
Hauser, SS-Sturmbannführer Hans, 136–40
Hauser, SS-Obergruppenführer Paul, 85, 140
Heidrich, Generalmajor Richard, 123
Hermann, Oberleutnant Harry, 47–50
Hochgartz, Major Günther, 94–7
Hug, Obergefreiter Eduard, 113–14

J
Jamrowski, Major Siegfried, 101–4

K
Karck, SS-Hauptsturmführer, 84–8
Keese, Major Heinrich, 119–20
Kepplinger, SS-Sturmbannführer Ludwig, 45–7
Kesselring, Generalfeldmarschall Albert, 71, 99
Kleinheisterkamp, SS-Obergruppenfüher Matthias, 135
Koch, Major Walter, 34, 51
Krass, SS-Obersturmbannführer Hugo, 86
Kübler, Generalmajor Ludwig, 37

L
Leeb, Generalfeldmarschall Wilhelm, 67
Lepkowski, Oberleutnant Erich, 106, 107, 108, 109
Liebling, Oberstleutnant Paul, 125, 126, 127, 128
Luftwaffe Units:
1 Fallschirm Division, 49, 98–9, 102, 123
2 Fallschirm Division, 49, 78, 102, 107

5 Fallschirm Division, 112
6 Fallschirm Division, 36, 50, 53, 126
7 Fallschirm Division, 53, 100
8 Fallschirm Division, 53
Fallschirm Flak Abteilung 2, 76
Fallschirm Flak Maschinengewehr Bataillon, 76
Fallschirm Korps Pioniere Bataillon, 35, 36
I Fallschirm Korps, 124
II Fallschirm Korps, 53
Fallschirm Panzer Jagd Brigade Herrmann, 50
Fallschirm Panzer Jager Abteilung 2, 76
Fallschirm Panzer Korps Hermann Göring, 48
Fallschirm Sturm Abteilung Koch, 33
Fallschirmjäger Lehr Bataillon, 49
Fallschirmjäger Lehr Regiment 21, 49
Fallschirmjäger Regiment 1, 33, 34, 99, 111
Fallschirmjäger Regiment 2, 106–8
Fallschirmjäger Regiment 3, 66–7, 97–9, 101–2, 111–12, 122
Fallschirmjäger Regiment 4, 99
Fallschirmjäger Regiment 15, 112
Fallschirmjäger Regiment 16, 53
Fallschirmjäger Regiment 17, 53
Fallschirmjäger Regiment 18, 36, 53
Fallschirmjäger Ski Bataillon, 122
Fallschirmjäger Sturm Regiment 1, 35, 51
Fallschirmschule 1, 76
Fallschirmschule Stendal, 48, 66
Flieger Ausbildungs Regiment 82, 75
7 Flieger Division, 48, 51–2, 67, 97, 101–2, 112, 122–3
XI Flieger Korps, 49
Fliegerschule Staaken, 50
Landespolizeigruppe General Göring, 48
Legion Condor, 50, 57
Luftlande Sturm Regiment, 66
1 Luftwaffe Feld Division, 126
Luftwaffe Kriegsschule Gatow, 68, 76

M
Meindl, General Eugen, 52, 66
Meyer, Major Heinz, 111–13
Meyer, SS-Oberführer Kurt, 104
Michael, Major Georg, 29–33
Mischke, Hauptmann Gerd, 75–7

N

Neumann, Oberstabsarzt Dr.
Heinrich, 50, 51

P

Plocher, Generalmajor Hermann, 53
Pössinger, Major Michael, 36–40
Preiss, SS-Brigadeführer Gerd, 88

R

Reber, SS-Obersturmführer
Gustav-Peter, 134–6
Richter, SS-Sturmbannführer
Friedrich, 130–4
Ringel, Generalleutnant Julius, 51,
107
Rohr, Generalmajor, 63

S

Sandig, SS-Obersturmbannführer
Rudolf, 85
Sassen, Leutnant Bruno, 66–9
Schellong, SS-Obersturmbannführer
Conrad, 84
Schrijnen, SS-Unterscharführer Remi,
82–4
Schneidereit, SS-Untersturmführer
Alfred, 89
Springer, SS-Sturmbannführer
Heinrich, 104
Stadler, SS-Brigadeführer Sylvester,
59
Steglich, Oberst Martin, 72–5
Student, General Kurt, 34–5
Sturm, Leutnant Hans, 59–65

U

Ullrich, SS-Oberführer Karl, 56–8

V

Von Bostell, Oberleutnant Wolfgang,
114–18
Von Vietinghoff-Scheel, General
Heinrich-Gottfried, 99
Vogt, SS-Sturmbannführer Fritz, 40–4

W

Waffen-SS Units:
8 SS-Freiwilligen Kavallerie Division
Florian Geyer, 58
22 SS-Freiwilligen Kavallerie Division
Maria Theresia, 58

SS-Freiwilligen Panzer Grenadier
Regiment 48 General Seyffardt, 43
SS-Freiwilligen Panzer Grenadier
Regiment 23 Norge, 42, 44
23 SS-Freiwilligen Panzer Grenadier
Division Nederland, 43
27 SS-Freiwilligen Panzer Grenadier
Division Langemark, 82
SS-Freiwilligen Legion Flandern, 82
IX SS-Gebirgs Korps, 43
III SS-(Germanisches) Panzer Korps:
SS-Junkerschule Braunschweig, 40,
56, 131, 136
SS-Junkerschule Kienschlag, 135
SS-Junkerschule Tölz, 42
SS-Kraftfahrtechnischen Lehranstalt
der Waffen-SS, 42
Leibstandarte SS Adolf Hitler, 84–5,
88, 91, 104, 130, 134
2 SS-Panzer Division Das Reich, 42,
131–2, 139–40
3 SS-Panzer Division Totenkopf, 42,
56–8
5 SS-Panzer Division Wiking, 43–4,
46, 58–9
9 SS-Panzer Division Frundsberg, 59
10 SS-Panzer Division Frundsberg,
132
12 SS-Panzer Division Hitler Jugend,
104–5
17 SS-Panzer Grenadier Division
Götz von Berlichingen, 46, 112
SS-Panzer Grenadier Regiment 5, 57
SS-Panzer Grenadier Regiment 6
Theodor Eicke, 58
SS-Panzer Grenadier Regiment 21,
132
SS-Panzer Grenadier Regiment 22,
132
SS-Polizei Division, 137
schwere SS-Panzer Abteilung 102,
129
schwere SS-Panzer Abteilung 502,
135
SS-Standarte Deutschland, 40, 45,
131–2, 136
SS-Standarte Der Führer, 45, 132
SS-Sturmbrigade Langemark, 82
SS-Unterführerschule Lauenberg, 42
SS-Verfügungs Division, 40, 56, 131
SS-Verfügungstruppe, 40, 45, 56
33 Waffen-Grenadier Division der SS
Charlemagne, 30

Weber, Obergefreiter Franz, 109–11
Wegener, Leutnant Wilhelm, 78–81
Weidinger, SS-Obersturmbannführer
   Otto, 140

Witt, SS-Brigadeführer Fritz, 104
Witzig, Major Rudolf, 33–4
Wunsche, SS-Obersturmbannführer
   Max, 104–5